THE HEALING POWER OF
FLOWERS

THE HEALING POWER OF

FLOWERS

EXPLORING BACH FLOWER REMEDIES

Authored By,

Supriya Salve

Disclaimer

This book has been published with all reasonable efforts taken to make the material error-free after the consent of the author. This book is sold subject to the condition that it shall not, by way of trade or otherwise, be lent, resold, or otherwise circulated without the copyright owner's prior written consent in any form of binding or cover other than that in which it is published and without a similar condition including this condition being imposed on the subsequent purchaser and without limiting the rights under copyright reserved above, no part of this publication maybe reproduced, stored in or introduced into a retrieval system or transmitted in any form or by any other means without the permission of the copyright owner.

Registered Office- 907-Sneh Nagar, Sapna Sangeeta Road, Agrasen Square, Indore – 452001 (M.P.), India

Website: http://www.wingspublication.com

Email: mybook@wingspublication.com

First Published by WINGS PUBLICATION 2024

Copyright © Supriya Salve

Title : The Healing Power of Flowers

Price : Rs. 799 I AED 50 I $ 15

All Rights Reserved.

ISBN : 978-93-6006-281-1

LIMITS OF LIABILITY/DISCLAIMER OF WARRANTY

The Healing Power of Flowers

Exploring Bach Flower Remedies

Dedication

In the symphony of life, there are threads of gratitude of life and strands of inspiration that weave our stories. This book, **"The Healing Power of Flowers,"** stands as a testament to the beautiful connections that have shaped its creation.

To the divine presence that guides us through the intricate garden of existence, I humbly dedicate this work to God, the source of all healing and harmony. May the essence of the flowers within these pages bloom as a reflection of Gods grace.

To **Guru Dattatreya**, whose wisdom and spiritual guidance have been a beacon of light on my journey.

Wings Publication has been the wind beneath my wings, lifting this endeavor to new heights. **Dr. Kailash** and **Dr. Deepak Prab**, your support and belief in the power of this message have been invaluable. Without your invisible support, this book would not have blossomed so beautifully.

In acknowledgment and deep appreciation, I extend my gratitude to these divine forces and dedicated individuals. Without them, this literary bouquet would not have come to fruition so soon.

With heartfelt thanks,

Supriya Salve

Edward Bach began his medical studies in Birmingham and later
Edward Bach began his medical studies in Birmingham and later continued at the University College Hospital in London, where he served as a House Surgeon. He also established a private practice with consulting rooms on Harley Street. In addition to his medical work, he delved into bacteriology and pathology, conducting original research on vaccines in his own laboratory.

Dr. Edward Bach successfully qualified as a doctor in 1912. Upon receiving his diplomas, he remarked, "It will take me five years to unlearn all that I have been taught."

In 1917, Dr. Bach was caring for soldiers who had returned injured from France. One day, he experienced a severe haemorrhage and was rushed into an operating theatre. His colleagues performed surgery to remove a tumour, but the prognosis was bleak. After regaining consciousness, Bach was informed that he had only three months left to live.

As soon as he was physically able, Bach returned to his laboratory with the intention of advancing his work as much as possible in the limited time he believed he had left. However, as weeks passed, he began to regain strength, and the three-month prognosis came and went, finding him in better health than ever. He attributed his recovery to a strong sense of purpose, as he still had important work to complete.

This information provides an overview of Dr. Edward Bach's medical education, research interests, and personal experience that led him to pursue his later work in alternative medicine, specifically the development of Bach flower remedies.

Acknowledgements

Honoring Dr. Edward Bach

In the pursuit of knowledge and the exploration of healing modalities, we often stand on the shoulders of visionaries who have paved the way for our understanding. In the world of holistic health and emotional well-being, one such visionary is Dr. Edward Bach.

As we journeyed through the intricate world of Bach Flower Remedies and explored the profound impact they have on our emotional health, we were constantly reminded of Dr. Bach's pioneering spirit and unwavering dedication to the betterment of humanity.

We extend our deepest gratitude and acknowledgement to Dr. Edward Bach for his invaluable contributions to the field of natural healing. His deep connection to nature, his profound insight into the human psyche, and his tireless efforts to distil the essence of healing from the petals of flowers have left an indelible mark on the world.

Dr. Bach's remedies, born from his deep love for nature and his unwavering commitment to alleviating human suffering, continue to touch the lives of countless individuals worldwide. His legacy lives on in the gentle cadence of each flower's essence and in the hearts of those who have found solace, balance, and transformation through his work.

We also acknowledge the practitioners, researchers, and advocates who have carried Dr. Bach's legacy forward, sharing his remedies with the world and tirelessly promoting emotional well-being. Their dedication to the healing power of flowers is a testament to the enduring impact of Dr. Bach's vision.

To all the individuals who have embraced Bach Flower Remedies as a path to emotional harmony and healing, we extend our heartfelt appreciation. Your openness to explore and your willingness to embrace the wisdom of nature are a testament to the timeless relevance of Dr. Bach's remedies.

Finally, we acknowledge you, the reader, for embarking on this journey of exploration and self-discovery with us. It is our hope that the insights shared within these pages will inspire you to carry the torch of emotional well-being forward, just as Dr. Edward Bach did in his time.

With deepest gratitude and a profound sense of reverence, we dedicate this work to the memory and legacy of Dr. Edward Bach, whose wisdom and compassion continue to touch the lives of those who seek healing through the gentle power of flowers.

The Bach Centre The Bach Centre house, Mount Vernon, in Brightwell-cum-Sotwell, Oxfordshire, is owned today by a Registered Charity controlled by the Ramsell family set up by John Ramsell in 1989

Supriya Salve's book titled "The Healing Power of Flowers: Exploring Bach Flower Remedies."

Supriya Salve, an Emotional Well-being Coach, was inspired to write her book "The Healing Power of Flowers: Exploring Bach Flower Remedies" after witnessing a remarkable transformation in one of her clients, Neeta.

Neeta had been struggling with chronic anxiety and self-doubt for years. Her fear of public speaking had held her back both professionally and personally. She had missed out on numerous opportunities and felt trapped in a cycle of anxiety and missed chances.

One day, Neeta decided to seek help and came across Supriya's coaching services. Supriya, with her expertise in Bach Flower Remedies, began working closely with Neeta to address her deep-rooted fears and insecurities.

Over the course of several months, Neeta underwent a profound change. With Supriya's guidance, she started using specific Bach Flower Remedies tailored to her emotional needs. As she diligently incorporated these remedies into her daily routine, she noticed a gradual but significant shift in her emotional well-being.

Neeta's transformation was nothing short of remarkable. She not only overcame her fear of public speaking but also found newfound confidence in all aspects of her life. She began excelling in her career, taking on leadership roles, and even started mentoring others who struggled with similar anxieties.

Impressed by the power of Bach Flower Remedies and Supriya's guidance, Neeta suggested that Supriya should share her knowledge and experiences with a broader audience. She believed that countless individuals out there could benefit from these natural remedies and the insights Supriya had to offer.

This heartwarming success story inspired Supriya Salve to write her book, "The Healing Power of Flowers." In the book, she not only recounts Neeta's transformation but also delves into the world of Bach Flower Remedies, providing practical guidance on how anyone can use these remedies to enhance their emotional well-being.

Through Neeta's journey, readers are encouraged to explore the profound impact that Bach Flower Remedies can have on their own lives. Supriya's book is not just a collection of remedies but a source of hope and inspiration for those seeking to conquer their emotional challenges and live life to the fullest.

"The Healing Power of Flowers" is a testament to the incredible transformation that is possible when one taps into the natural healing energies of Bach Flower Remedies. It serves as a motivating call to action for readers to embark on their own journeys of emotional healing and personal growth.

Why should someone consider using Bach Flower Remedies instead of other remedies available in the market for emotional well-being?"

Using Bach Flower Remedies offers a unique and holistic approach to emotional and mental well-being, and there are several reasons why individuals may choose Bach Flower Remedies over other remedies available in the market:

1. **Natural and Safe: Bach** Flower Remedies are completely natural and safe. They are made from the essence of wildflowers and are non-toxic. They do not carry the risk of side effects or addiction often associated with pharmaceutical medications.

2. **Holistic Approach:** Bach Flower Remedies address emotional and mental imbalances, focusing on the root causes of emotional issues rather than just alleviating symptoms. They consider the mind-body connection, promoting overall wellness.

3. **Personalized Treatment:** Bach Flower Remedies are selected based on an individual's unique emotional state. This personalized approach ensures that the remedy is tailored to the specific emotions and concerns of the person.

4. **Gentle and Non-Invasive:** Bach Flower Remedies are

gentle and non-invasive. They can be used alongside other treatments, including conventional medicine, without interfering with their efficacy.

5. **Emotional Resilience:** Bach Flower Remedies aim to build emotional resilience, helping individuals better cope with life's challenges, stressors, and emotional ups and downs. They support emotional growth and self-awareness.

6. **No Known Interactions:** unlike some herbal remedies and supplements, Bach Flower Remedies have no known negative interactions with medications or other treatments. This makes them suitable for a wide range of individuals.

7. **Versatility:** Bach Flower Remedies can be used for various emotional concerns, including anxiety, fear, anger, sadness, and more. This versatility allows for a comprehensive approach to emotional wellness.

8. **Self-Help:** Bach Flower Remedies are accessible for self-help. Individuals can learn to select remedies for themselves or consult with a practitioner for guidance. This empowers individuals to take an active role in their emotional well-being.

9. **Complementary to Other Therapies:** They can complement other holistic therapies, such as acupuncture, aromatherapy, meditation, and yoga, enhancing the overall effectiveness of a holistic wellness plan.

10. **Historical Success:** Bach Flower Remedies have a history of successful use dating back to the 1930s when they were developed by Dr. Edward Bach. Their continued popularity and positive testimonials speak to their effectiveness.

While other remedies and therapies are available in the market, Bach Flower Remedies stand out for their gentle yet profound impact on emotional well-being. Their unique approach, individualized selection, and holistic focus make them a valuable tool for those seeking to achieve emotional balance and resilience.

Preface

The Healing Power of Flowers - Exploring Bach Flower Remedies

Welcome to a journey that takes us back to nature, to the soothing embrace of flowers, and to the profound world of Bach Flower Remedies. In the pages of this book, we embark on a voyage of discovery, guided by the belief that the healing power of nature is a source of profound well-being.

The world we live in today is filled with remarkable advances in science and medicine, yet there remains an enduring wisdom in the simplicity of nature. Dr. Edward Bach, a visionary physician and researcher, recognized this timeless truth when he introduced the world to Bach Flower Remedies. His work revolutionized holistic healing by harnessing the gentle yet potent healing properties of flowers.

Our motivation to write this book arises from a profound respect for the wisdom of Dr. Bach and a deep appreciation for the healing potential found in the heart of nature. Bach Flower Remedies are not just tinctures derived from flowers; they are pathways to emotional balance, catalysts for personal transformation, and keys to unlocking the harmony that resides within us all.

The journey we embark upon through these pages is multifaceted. It is an exploration of the principles and philosophy that underpin Bach's Flower Remedies, delving into the understanding of emotions, personality, and the mind-body connection. It is a practical guide, providing insights into the remedies themselves, their applications, and methods of administration. But, most importantly, it is an invitation to a deeper level of self-awareness, self-care, and healing.

We recognize that in the complex tapestry of modern life, emotional well-being often takes a backseat to the demands of our busy schedules and the allure of quick fixes. Yet, we believe that investing in our emotional health is one of the most profound acts of self-care we can undertake.

As you read these pages and explore the world of Bach Flower Remedies, we encourage you to approach this journey with an open heart and a curious mind. Whether you are new to the world of natural healing or an experienced practitioner, there is always more to discover, more wisdom to unearth, and more healing to experience.

In this book, you will find not only information but also an invitation to connect with the essence of flowers, to understand the subtle energies that surround us, and to explore the intricate dance of emotions within your own being. You will discover how Bach Flower Remedies can support your journey toward emotional balance, harmony, and personal growth.

This is a journey of healing and empowerment, a journey where the flowers become your allies, and nature becomes your guide. It is our hope that the insights and knowledge shared within these pages will inspire you to embrace the healing power of flowers and to embark on a transformative journey toward greater emotional well-being and wholeness.

Table Of Contents

"Harmony of Healing: Dr. Edward Bach's Remedies"

Where healing thrives, Dr. Edward Bach's remedies arrive.
A symphony of flowers, nature's song,
Restoring balance when emotions go wrong.

Agrimony's note, for hidden pain,
Releasing the mask, embracing the strain.
Aspen whispers, calming fears unknown,
A gentle melody, seeds of peace sown.

Beech's rhythm, fostering tolerance true,
Harmonizing hearts, a compassionate view.
Centaury's tune, setting boundaries strong,
Empowering souls to where they belong.

Cerato's melody, intuition's guide,
Trusting the whispers, with confidence stride.
Cherry Plum's harmony, dispelling fear,
A calming cadence, serenity near.

Chestnut Bud's rhythm, learning anew,
Breaking patterns, embracing what's true.
Chicory's chorus, love's tender embrace,
Letting go, granting freedom and space.

Clematis' song, Dreams Taking Flight,
Grounded visions, shining ever so bright.
Crab Apple's symphony, cleansing the soul,
Releasing burdens, making spirits whole.

Elm's rhythm, lifting burdens untold,
A symphony of strength to unfold.
Gentian's melody, dispelling despair,
Infusing hope, filling the air.

Gorse's refrain, reigniting faith's fire,
Guiding through the darkness, lifting spirits higher.
Heather's harmony, a listening ear,
Sharing compassion, removing all fear.

Holly's rhythm, love's fierce flame,
Transforming hate, kindling a gentle aim.
Honeysuckle's tune, releasing the past,
Living in the present, where joy's shadows are cast.

Hornbeam's melody, weary souls restore,
Renewing energy, like an ocean's roar.
Impatiens' rhythm, soothing impatience's sting,
Embracing patience, the peace it brings.

Larch's symphony, confidence's rise,
Banishing doubt, reaching for the skies.

Mimulus' refrain, known fears erased,
Courageous steps were taken, with fears effaced.

Mustard's tune, dispelling gloom's embrace,
A ray of sunlight, bringing joy's grace.
Oak's rhythm, tireless strength renewed,
Balancing rest, energy pursued.

Olive's melody rejuvenates hearts and minds,
Restoring vitality, where weariness unwinds.
Pine's refrain, forgiveness is freely given,
Embracing self-love, where hearts are driven.

Red Chestnut's rhythm, worry's release,
Trusting in love, finding inner peace.
Rock Rose's melody, banishing terror's fright,
Courage awakened, shining in the darkest night.

Rock Water's tune, rigid ideals unbind,
Flowing with life, an open-hearted mind.
Scleranthus' rhythm, decisions made clear,
Finding balance, stepping without fear.

Star of Bethlehem's symphony, healing's embrace,
Bringing solace, peace in its grace.
Sweet Chestnut's melody, anguish transformed,
Awakening hope, where new horizons formed.

Vervain's rhythm, zealous hearts appeased,
Harmonizing passion, finding inner ease.
Vine's refrain, leadership guided by love,
Nurturing souls like a gentle dove.

Walnut's tune, navigating life's change,
Embracing transformation, a melody so strange.
Water Violet's melody, solitude's embrace,
Connecting with others, hearts intertwined in grace.

White Chestnut's rhythm, quieting the mind,
Stillness within, tranquillity to find.
Wild Oat's symphony, purpose's thread,
Guiding dreams, where the heart is led.

Wild Rose's melody, passion reignited,
Reviving the spirit, where joy is invited.
Willow's refrain, releasing bitterness's hold,
Embracing forgiveness, a melody bold.

Together, they weave a harmonious sound,
Dr. Edward Bach's remedies abound.
In rhythm and rhyme, their healing power,
Restoring balance, each soul they empower.

Supriya salve

<u>**Chapter : 1**</u>

Introduction

"Health depends on being in harmony with our souls."
- Dr. Edward Bach.

This quote encapsulates Dr. Edward Bach's holistic approach to healing, emphasizing the interconnectedness of physical health, emotional well-being, and the soul's harmony. Bach believed that true health could only be achieved when these elements were in balance and alignment. His work with Bach Flower Remedies was dedicated to helping individuals restore this essential harmony within themselves.

- **Dr. Edward Bach: The Man and His Mission**

Dr. Edward Bach was a renowned British physician, bacteriologist, and homoeopath who made significant contributions to the field of alternative medicine. Born on September 24, 1886, in Moseley, Birmingham, England, Bach dedicated his life to understanding the connection between emotional well-being and physical health. His pioneering work in the development of flower essences has had a lasting impact on holistic healing practices.

Bach's journey began with a successful career in conventional medicine. He obtained his medical degree from the University College Hospital in London and worked as a house surgeon and casualty medical officer. However, he became disillusioned with the limitations of mainstream medicine, which focused primarily on treating symptoms rather than addressing the root causes of illness.

Driven by a deep desire to find a more holistic approach to healing, Bach explored various avenues. He studied immunology, which led him to his work as a bacteriologist. He made notable advancements in this field, including the creation of vaccines and the discovery of bowel nosodes. Despite these achievements, Bach felt that he had not yet found the key to true healing.

It was during this period of self-discovery that Bach embarked on a transformative journey. He began to observe the healing properties of plants and became convinced that nature held the answers he sought. He believed that by harnessing the essence of certain flowers, he could tap into their inherent healing energies and restore balance to the human body.

Bach dedicated years to researching and developing his flower remedies. He identified a total of 38 different flowers, each with unique healing properties corresponding to specific emotional imbalances. The remedies he created were designed to address negative emotional states such as fear, anxiety, anger, and despair, which he believed were at the core of many physical ailments.

Bach's approach to healing was profoundly simple and gentle. He believed that true healing occurred when individuals re-established harmony within themselves. His remedies, known as Bach flower essences, were prepared by infusing flowers in water and capturing their energetic essence. These remedies were safe, non-toxic, and could be used by people of all ages, including children and pets.

Bach's mission was not solely focused on developing remedies but also on empowering individuals to take charge of their own health. He believed that each person had the innate ability to understand their emotional needs and select the appropriate remedy to restore balance. Bach encouraged people to reconnect with nature, listen to their intuition, and trust their own healing journey.

The impact of Dr. Bach's work continues to resonate with millions of people worldwide. His flower remedies have gained widespread recognition and are used by practitioners in various healing modalities, including homoeopathy, naturopathy, and holistic medicine. The simplicity and accessibility of the remedies have made them accessible to individuals seeking natural alternatives for their physical and emotional well-being.

Dr. Edward Bach's legacy extends beyond his remedies. His teachings emphasize the importance of treating the individual as a whole recognizing the interconnectedness of mind, body, and spirit. His holistic approach paved the way for a paradigm shift in healthcare, inspiring countless individuals to explore complementary and alternative healing modalities.

In conclusion, Dr. Edward Bach was a visionary pioneer in the field of alternative medicine. Through his research, he discovered the profound healing potential of flower essences and created a system that addressed the emotional roots of illness. His mission to empower individuals to take control of their health and reconnect with nature continues to inspire and transform lives. Dr. Bach's work serves as a testament to the enduring power of holistic healing and the remarkable potential of the human spirit.

- ## **The Philosophy and Principles of Bach Flower Remedies**

Bach Flower Remedies is a form of alternative medicine developed by Dr. Edward Bach in the early 20th century. It is based on the belief that emotional and psychological imbalances are the underlying causes of physical illness. Bach Flower Remedies aim to restore emotional harmony and promote overall well-being. The philosophy and principles of Bach Flower Remedies revolve around the holistic approach to healing and the understanding of the connection between emotions and health.

Dr. Edward Bach, a British physician and homoeopath, believed that the root cause of illness lies in the disharmony between the soul or the higher self and the personality. According to Bach, negative emotions such as fear, anger, and worry disrupt the natural flow of vital energy in the body, leading to physical and mental ailments. He believed that by addressing these emotional imbalances, true healing could be achieved.

The Bach Flower Remedies consist of 38 different flower essences, each corresponding to a specific emotional state or personality trait. These essences are prepared by infusing flowers in spring water and then preserving them in a solution of brandy. The remedies work by subtly influencing the individual's emotional state, bringing about a positive shift in their outlook and restoring emotional balance.

The principles of Bach Flower Remedies are based on simplicity, gentleness, and individualization. The remedies are safe and non-toxic, making them suitable for people of all ages, including children and pets. They are believed to work in harmony with other forms of treatment and do not interfere with conventional medication.

One of the key principles of Bach Flower Remedies is the notion that each person is unique and has their own specific emotional needs. Rather than focusing on the symptoms of a disease, the remedies address the underlying emotional state of the individual. For example, someone experiencing excessive worry and anxiety may benefit from the essence of Rock Rose, while someone dealing with feelings of despondency and hopelessness may find relief in the essence of Sweet Chestnut.

Another principle of Bach Flower Remedies is self-help and self-awareness. Dr. Bach believed that individuals have the capacity to understand and heal themselves. The remedies act as a tool for self-reflection, helping individuals to become more aware of their emotions and to take responsibility for their own well-being. By identifying and addressing their emotional imbalances, individuals can work towards personal growth and a greater sense of harmony.

Bach Flower Remedies also emphasize the importance of prevention rather than cure. Dr. Bach believed that by maintaining emotional balance, individuals can prevent the development of physical illness. The remedies can be used proactively to support emotional well-being during times of stress, change, or transition.

In conclusion, the philosophy and principles of Bach Flower Remedies revolve around the belief that emotional imbalances are at the root of physical illness. The remedies aim to restore emotional harmony and promote overall well-being by addressing specific emotional states and personality traits. The principles of simplicity, gentleness, individualization, self-help, and prevention guide the practice of Bach Flower Remedies. By understanding and addressing their emotions, individuals can work towards healing, personal growth, and a greater sense of inner harmony.

- **Understanding Emotional Well-being and its Importance**

Emotional well-being refers to the overall state of an individual's emotional health and happiness. It encompasses a person's ability to manage their emotions effectively, cope with stress, maintain positive relationships, and experience a sense of fulfilment and purpose in life. Understanding and nurturing emotional well-being is of utmost importance as it has a profound impact on one's overall quality of life. In this book, I will explain the concept of emotional well-being, its significance, and strategies to enhance and maintain it.

Emotional well-being plays a crucial role in our daily lives. When we are emotionally healthy, we are better equipped to handle life's challenges, adapt to changes, and maintain positive relationships. It provides us with a solid foundation for personal growth, resilience, and overall happiness. On the other hand, poor emotional well-being can lead to a range of negative outcomes, such as increased stress, anxiety, depression, and difficulty in forming and maintaining meaningful connections with others.

One of the key aspects of emotional well-being is self-awareness. It involves recognizing and understanding our own emotions, needs, and desires. Self-awareness allows us to identify and manage our emotions effectively, make informed decisions, and take actions that align with our values and goals. It also enables us to have a deeper understanding of others' emotions and perspectives, fostering empathy and strengthening interpersonal relationships.

Another important aspect is emotional resilience, which refers to our ability to bounce back from setbacks, adapt to change, and thrive in the face of adversity. Resilience is not about avoiding negative emotions or denying difficult situations; rather, it involves developing healthy coping mechanisms, seeking support when needed, and maintaining a positive outlook in the midst of challenges. Resilient individuals are better equipped to handle stress, maintain a balanced perspective, and find creative solutions to problems.

Positive relationships and social connections are also vital for emotional well-being. Humans are social beings, and we thrive when we have meaningful connections with others. Strong social support networks provide a sense of belonging, validation, and emotional nourishment. They offer a safe space to share our thoughts and feelings, seek guidance and support, and celebrate our successes. Cultivating and nurturing positive relationships can significantly enhance our emotional well-being.

Furthermore, engaging in activities that bring joy, purpose, and fulfilment is essential for emotional well-being. These activities, often referred to as "self-care," can vary from person to person and may include hobbies, exercise, spending time in nature, practising mindfulness or meditation, pursuing creative outlets, or simply spending quality time with loved ones. Taking time for self-care allows us to recharge, reduce stress, and reconnect with ourselves on a deeper level.

The importance of emotional well-being extends beyond the individual level. It has implications for society as a whole. Emotionally healthy individuals are more productive, engaged, and empathetic, contributing positively to their communities and workplaces. They are also more likely to exhibit pro-social behaviours, such as kindness, compassion, and altruism. Prioritizing emotional well-being on a societal level can lead to healthier and more harmonious communities.

To enhance and maintain emotional well-being, there are several strategies that individuals can adopt. Firstly, practising self-care on a regular basis is very important. This involves setting aside time for activities that promote relaxation, self-reflection, and personal growth. Engaging in physical exercise, eating a balanced diet, getting enough sleep, and managing stress effectively are also important factors in maintaining emotional well-being.

Additionally, seeking support from trusted individuals or professionals can be beneficial. Sharing our thoughts and feelings with a close friend, family member, or therapist can provide a fresh perspective, validation, and guidance. Developing a strong support network and being open to seeking help when needed is a sign of strength, not weakness.

Moreover, cultivating emotional intelligence is essential for enhancing emotional well-being. Emotional intelligence involves being aware of and managing our own emotions, as well as recognizing and understanding the emotions of others.

Developing skills such as empathy, active listening, and effective communication can greatly improve our relationships and overall emotional well-being.

In conclusion, emotional well-being is crucial for leading a fulfilling and meaningful life. It encompasses self-awareness, emotional resilience, positive relationships, and engaging in activities that bring joy and fulfilment. Prioritizing emotional well-being not only benefits individuals but also has far-reaching positive effects on society. By practising self-care, seeking support, and developing emotional intelligence, we can enhance and maintain our emotional well-being, leading to a healthier and happier life.

<u>**Chapter : 2**</u>

The Basics of Bach Flower Remedies

"I hope that one day the medical profession will turn from poisonous drugs to the study of nature and that the use of drugs will be discontinued except in cases of actual necessity."
Dr. Edward Bach.

This quote reflects Dr. Edward Bach's belief in the healing power of nature and his conviction that the study of natural remedies, such as Bach Flower Remedies, could offer gentler and more holistic approaches to health and emotional well-being compared to traditional pharmaceutical drugs.

Bach Flower Remedies, also known as Bach Flower Essences, is a form of alternative medicine that aims to balance emotional well-being. Developed by Dr. Edward Bach in the 1930s, these remedies are made from the essence of flowers and plants and are believed to address the underlying emotional imbalances that may contribute to physical and mental health issues. In this chapter, I will explain the basics of Bach Flower Remedies and how they are used.

Dr. Edward Bach was a British physician and homoeopath who believed that emotional disharmony was the root cause of many illnesses. He identified 38 different flowers and plants, each corresponding to a specific emotional state or personality trait. Bach believed that by addressing these emotional imbalances, a person's overall health and well-being could be restored.

The process of creating Bach Flower Remedies involves extracting the essence of flowers and plants through a gentle method known as "sun potentization." This method involves placing freshly picked flowers or plants in a glass bowl filled with spring water and allowing them to sit in the sun for several hours. The energy and healing properties of the flowers are believed to be transferred into the water, creating the essence.

Once the essence is prepared, it is preserved using brandy or a similar alcohol-based solution. The preserved essence is then diluted further and sold as individual remedies. Each Bach Flower Remedy is associated with a specific emotional state or personality trait, such as fear, anxiety, sadness, or lack of confidence.

To determine which Bach Flower Remedies are appropriate for an individual, a practitioner or the individual themselves can conduct a consultation or self-assessment. During this process, the person's emotional state, personality traits, and current challenges are considered. Based on this information, a personalized combination of remedies is created.

The remedies are typically taken orally, either directly from the stock bottle or diluted in water. A few drops of the remedy or a few sprays from a spray bottle are taken several times a day, depending on the individual's needs. The idea is that the essences work energetically to rebalance the emotions and restore a sense of well-being.

It is important to note that Bach Flower Remedies are not intended to replace medical treatment or professional mental health care. They are considered complementary therapies and are often used alongside conventional medicine. If you have a serious medical condition or mental health issue, it is essential to consult with a qualified healthcare professional.

One of the key principles of Bach Flower Remedies is the belief that emotional well-being is closely connected to physical health. By addressing emotional imbalances, it is thought that the body's natural healing mechanisms can be activated, leading to improved overall health.

Critics of Bach Flower Remedies argue that the efficacy of these remedies is primarily due to the placebo effect. However, proponents believe that the essences work on a subtle, energetic level, bringing about emotional shifts that can positively impact a person's well-being.

While scientific evidence for the effectiveness of Bach Flower Remedies is limited, many individuals report experiencing positive effects from using them. It is important to approach these remedies with an open mind and to remember that they may work differently for each person.

In conclusion, Bach Flower Remedies offers a unique approach to emotional well-being and healing. They are based on the belief that addressing emotional imbalances can have a positive impact on overall health. While their efficacy is debated, many people find them helpful in promoting emotional balance and personal growth. If you are interested in trying Bach Flower Remedies, it is recommended to consult with a qualified practitioner to determine the most appropriate remedies for your needs.

- **Overview of the 38 Bach Flower Remedies**

Bach Flower Remedies are a form of alternative medicine that was developed by Dr. Edward Bach in the 1930s. There are 38 different remedies, each made from the flowers of specific plants. These remedies are believed to restore emotional balance and address underlying negative emotions that may be causing physical or mental health issues. Here is an overview of the 38 Bach Flower Remedies:

1. Agrimony: For those who hide their inner troubles behind a cheerful facade.

2. Aspen: For unknown fears and apprehensions.

3. Beech: For individuals who are overly critical and intolerant.

4. Centaury: For people who have difficulty saying no and tend to be submissive.

5. Cerato: For those who lack confidence in their own judgment and constantly seek advice from others.

6. Cherry Plum: For fear of losing control or mental breakdown.

7. Chestnut Bud: For those who fail to learn from past experiences and repeat the same mistakes.

8. Chicory: For individuals who are possessive, demanding, and overly controlling.

9. Clematis: For daydreamers who are not fully engaged in the present.

10.   Crab Apple: For feelings of self-disgust and the need for purity and cleansing.

11.   Elm: For temporary feelings of being overwhelmed and burdened by responsibilities.

12.   Gentian: For discouragement and doubt after a setback.

13.   Gorse: For individuals who have lost hope and suffer from despair.

14.   Heather: For those who constantly talk about themselves and crave attention.

15.   Holly: For feelings of jealousy, envy, or suspicion.

16.   Honeysuckle: For individuals who are stuck in the past and have difficulty moving on.

17.   Hornbeam: For feelings of mental and physical fatigue, particularly upon starting a new task.

18.   Impatiens: For impatience, irritability, and a strong desire for things to happen quickly.

19.   Larch: For lack of confidence and fear of failure.

20.   Mimulus: For known fears and phobias, such as fear of heights or spiders.

21.   Mustard: For deep sadness and depression that comes and goes without any apparent reason.

22.   Oak: For persistent, hardworking individuals who push themselves beyond their limits.

23. Olive: For exhaustion, both mental and physical, after a long period of strain.

24. Pine: For feelings of guilt, self-blame, and self-criticism.

25. Red Chestnut: For excessive worry and fear for the well-being of others.

26. Rock Rose: For acute and extreme fear or terror.

27. Rock Water: For individuals who are strict, rigid, and set high standards for themselves.

28. Scleranthus: For indecisiveness and difficulty in making choices.

29. Star of Bethlehem: For shock, trauma, or emotional distress.

30. Sweet Chestnut: For feelings of extreme mental anguish and despair.

31. Vervain: For individuals who are highly strung, intense, and overenthusiastic.

32. Vine: For domineering, inflexible individuals who seek power and control over others.

33. Walnut: For times of transition or change, when one needs protection from outside influences.

34. Water Violet: For individuals who prefer to be alone, distant, and detached.

35. White Chestnut: For persistent, unwanted thoughts and mental arguments.

36.   Wild Oat: For individuals who feel unsure of their life's purpose and direction.

37.   Wild Rose: For apathy, resignation, and lack of interest in life.

38.   Willow: For individuals who harbour resentment, bitterness, and a sense of victimhood.

These remedies are typically taken orally, diluted in water or taken directly under the tongue. The appropriate remedies are chosen based on an individual's emotional state and specific needs. It's important to note that Bach Flower Remedies are not intended to replace medical treatment but rather to support emotional well-being. Consulting with a qualified healthcare professional is recommended for addressing physical or mental health concerns.

- **Preparation and Administration of Remedies**

Bach Flower Remedies are a form of alternative medicine that utilizes the healing properties of various flower essences. Developed by Dr. Edward Bach in the 1930s, these remedies aim to address emotional and psychological imbalances in individuals. There are 38 different Bach Flower Remedies, each targeting a specific emotional state or personality trait. In this article, we will discuss the preparation and administration of these remedies.

Preparation: The preparation of Bach Flower Remedies involves the extraction of the healing properties from specific flowers. Dr. Bach believed that the vibrational energy of the flowers could be captured in water and used to balance emotional states. The following steps outline the preparation process:

1. <u>Flower Selection</u>: Each Bach Flower Remedy corresponds to a specific flower or plant. The flowers are carefully selected based on their unique healing properties. For example, the Rock Rose flower essence is used for individuals experiencing terror or extreme fear, while the Impatiens flower essence is for those who are impatient and easily irritable.

2. <u>Sun Method:</u> The most common method of extraction is the "Sun Method." In this process, flower heads are placed in a clear glass bowl filled with spring water. The bowl is then left outside in direct sunlight for several hours. The energy of the sun is believed to infuse the water with the vibrational essence of the flowers.

3. <u>Boiling Method</u>: Some flowers, such as Heather or Impatiens, require the "Boiling Method" for extraction. The flowers are placed in a pot of water, which is then brought to a boil. After boiling for a short time, the water is strained, and the essence is obtained.

4. <u>Preservation:</u> Once the flower essences are extracted, they need to be preserved. The most common method of preservation is by adding brandy or grape-based alcohol to the essence. This mixture is known as the "mother tincture" and serves as the base for further dilution.

Administration: Bach Flower Remedies are typically taken orally, and the following guidelines can be followed for their administration:

1. <u>Selection of Remedies:</u> To determine which Bach Flower Remedies are suitable for an individual, it is important to assess their emotional state or personality traits. Dr. Bach categorized the remedies into seven groups: Fear, Uncertainty, Lack of Interest, Loneliness, Over-sensitivity, Despondency, and Overcare for Others. By identifying the primary emotional imbalance, the appropriate remedies can be selected.

2. <u>Single or Combination Remedies:</u> Bach Flower Remedies can be taken individually or in combination. In cases where multiple emotional states are present, a combination of remedies may be recommended. A maximum of six remedies can be mixed in a treatment bottle.

3. <u>Dilution:</u> The mother tincture is diluted before administration. Typically, two drops of the mother tincture are added to 30 ml (approximately one ounce) of water. This diluted mixture can be stored in a dropper bottle for regular use.

4. <u>Dosage and Frequency:</u> The standard dosage for Bach Flower Remedies is four drops four times a day. The drops can be taken directly on the tongue or added to a glass of water. In acute situations, the dosage can be increased every few minutes until relief is obtained.

5. <u>Duration of Treatment:</u> The duration of treatment with Bach Flower Remedies varies depending on the individual. Some individuals may experience

immediate relief, while others may require long-term use. Regular reassessment of emotional states can help determine the need for continued use.

It is important to note that Bach Flower Remedies are not a substitute for professional medical advice or treatment. They are intended to support emotional well-being and should be used in conjunction with appropriate medical care.

In conclusion, the preparation and administration of Bach Flower Remedies involve the careful selection and extraction of flower essences to address emotional imbalances. By following the prescribed methods, individuals can benefit from the healing properties of these remedies and promote emotional well-being.

- **Safety Guidelines and Precautions**

Bach Flower Remedies are a system of natural remedies developed by Dr. Edward Bach in the 1930s. These remedies are derived from flowers and plants and are believed to promote emotional and mental well-being. While Bach Flower Remedies are generally considered safe and gentle, it is essential to follow certain guidelines and take necessary precautions to ensure their proper and effective use. This article will provide you with 38 safety guidelines and precautions to keep in mind when using Bach Flower Remedies.

1. Consultation with a Qualified Practitioner: Before starting ny Bach Flower Remedy regimen, it is advisable to consult a qualified Bach Flower Remedy practitioner or a healthcare professional who is knowledgeable about these remedies. They can provide

personalized guidance based on your specific needs and conditions.

2. Proper Storage: Store Bach Flower Remedies in a cool, dry place, away from direct sunlight and strong odours. Keep them out of the reach of children and pets.

3. Allergy Testing: If you have a known sensitivity or allergy to flowers or plants, it is recommended to perform a patch test before using Bach Flower Remedies. Apply a small amount of the remedy on a small area of your skin and monitor for any adverse reactions.

4. Individual Remedy Selection: Bach Flower Remedies are selected based on specific emotional states and concerns. Take time to understand the remedies and their indications, and select the ones that best match your emotional needs.

5. Personalized Treatment Plans: Bach Flower Remedies work best when used in a personalized treatment plan. Work with a practitioner to develop a comprehensive plan that addresses your emotional well-being holistically.

6. Dosage and Administration: Follow the recommended dosage and administration guidelines provided by your practitioner or the product label. Bach Flower Remedies are typically taken orally, either directly or diluted in water.

7. Mixing Remedies: You can combine up to six different Bach Flower Remedies in a single treatment bottle. However, it is generally recommended to seek guidance from a practitioner for complex or long-standing emotional issues.

8. Avoid Contamination: Ensure that droppers or pipettes used to administer the remedies are clean and free from contamination. Avoid touching the dropper with your hands or tongue to prevent potential contamination.

9. Pregnancy and Breastfeeding: If you are pregnant or breastfeeding, consult your healthcare provider before using Bach Flower Remedies. While they are generally considered safe, it is important to ensure their suitability during these periods.

10. Medical Conditions and Medications: Inform your healthcare provider about any existing medical conditions or medications you are taking before using Bach Flower Remedies. They can help determine if there are any potential interactions or contraindications.

11. Emergency Situations: In emergency situations where immediate medical attention is required, Bach Flower Remedies should not be used as a substitute for professional medical care. Seek appropriate medical help promptly.

12. Children and Bach Flower Remedies: Bach Flower Remedies can be used for children, but it is advisable to

consult a practitioner who specializes in pediatric care. They can provide guidance on appropriate remedies and dosages for children.

13. Monitoring Progress: Regularly assess and monitor your progress while using Bach Flower Remedies. Keep track of any changes or improvements in your emotional well-being and discuss them with your practitioner.

14. Duration of Use: The duration of Bach Flower Remedy use varies depending on individual needs. Some individuals may benefit from short-term use, while others may require longer treatment periods. Discuss the duration of use with your practitioner.

15. Sensitivity to Alcohol: Bach Flower Remedies are preserved in a small amount of brandy, which acts as a natural preservative. If you are sensitive to alcohol, dilute the remedy in water or discuss alternatives with your practitioner.

16. Emotional Release: Bach Flower Remedies can sometimes trigger an emotional release or bring unresolved issues to the surface. Be prepared for this possibility and seek support if needed.

17. Not a Substitute for Professional Help: Bach Flower Remedies are not a substitute for professional mental health or medical care. If you have severe emotional distress or mental health conditions, seek appropriate

help from qualified professionals.

18. Discontinue if Adverse Reactions Occur: If you experience any adverse reactions or worsening of symptoms while using Bach Flower Remedies, discontinue their use and consult your healthcare provider or practitioner.

19. Quality and Authenticity: Ensure that you purchase Bach Flower Remedies from reputable sources to guarantee their quality and authenticity. Counterfeit or improperly prepared remedies may not have the desired effects.

20. Ethical Harvesting Practices: Support companies that follow ethical harvesting practices when sourcing flowers and plants for Bach Flower Remedies. Sustainable and environmentally conscious methods help preserve the integrity of these natural remedies.

Bach Flower Remedies can be valuable tools for promoting emotional well-being, but it is essential to use them safely and responsibly. By following these 38 safety guidelines and precautions, you can ensure that you derive the maximum benefits from Bach Flower Remedies while minimizing any potential risks. Remember to consult with a qualified practitioner and listen to your body's responses throughout your journey with Bach Flower Remedies.

Chapter : 3

Addressing Emotional Imbalances

> *There is no true healing unless there is a change in outlook,*
> *peace of mind and inner happiness.*
> - EDWARD BACH

Dr. Edward Bach's quote beautifully encapsulates his holistic approach to healing. He emphasized that genuine healing goes beyond just the alleviation of physical symptoms; it involves a profound transformation of one's inner state, fostering peace of mind, inner happiness, and a positive outlook on life. This holistic perspective underscores the importance of addressing emotional and mental well-being as integral components of overall health and healing.

Addressing emotional imbalances refers to the process of recognizing, acknowledging, and actively working towards restoring equilibrium and well-being in one's emotional state. It involves taking proactive steps to understand and address the underlying causes and triggers of emotional distress or instability.

Emotional imbalances can manifest in various ways, such as excessive stress, anxiety, depression, anger, or mood swings. These imbalances may arise due to a range of factors, including personal experiences, relationships, work or academic pressures, health issues, or external circumstances.

Addressing emotional imbalances involves several key aspects:

1.   Self-awareness: Recognizing and acknowledging one's

emotions and understanding their impact on thoughts, behaviours, and overall well-being.

2. Identification of triggers: Identifying the specific situations, events, or thought patterns that contribute to emotional imbalances.

3. Emotional regulation: Developing strategies to manage and regulate emotions effectively, such as practising relaxation techniques, engaging in mindfulness exercises, or seeking professional help when needed.

4. Healthy coping mechanisms: Developing healthy coping mechanisms to deal with stress, anxiety, or negative emotions, such as engaging in physical activity, seeking support from loved ones, pursuing hobbies, or practising self-care activities.

5. Seeking support: Knowing when to seek support from friends, family, or mental health professionals. It involves reaching out for guidance, validation, and assistance in navigating emotional challenges.

6. Balancing lifestyle factors: Paying attention to lifestyle factors that impact emotional well-being, such as maintaining a balanced diet, getting regular exercise, prioritizing sleep, and managing stress levels.

7. Addressing underlying issues: If emotional imbalances persist or become overwhelming, it may be necessary to explore and address underlying issues through therapy, counselling, or other forms of professional help.

The process of addressing emotional imbalances is unique to each individual, as everyone's experiences, triggers, and coping mechanisms differ. It requires self-reflection, self-care, and a commitment to personal growth and well-being.

By actively addressing emotional imbalances, individuals can develop greater emotional resilience, improve their overall mental health, and lead more fulfilling and balanced lives.

Let's consider the example of John, who leads a high-stress lifestyle due to the demands of his job and personal responsibilities.

John works in a demanding corporate job that requires long hours, tight deadlines, and frequent travel. On top of that, he is also a parent of two young children and takes care of his elderly parents. The accumulation of stress from work and personal life has taken a toll on his emotional well-being.

To address his stress lifestyle, John takes the following steps:

1. Self-awareness: John becomes aware of the physical and emotional signs of stress, such as fatigue, irritability, and difficulty concentrating. He acknowledges that his stress levels have reached an unsustainable point and need to be addressed.

2. Identifying triggers: John identifies specific triggers of stress, such as excessive workload, lack of time for self-care, difficulties in balancing work and family responsibilities, and the pressure to meet expectations in all areas of his life.

3. Time management and prioritization: John develops

effective time management strategies to better allocate his time and prioritize tasks. He sets realistic goals and breaks down big projects into smaller, manageable tasks. By doing so, he feels more in control and reduces the sense of being overwhelmed.

4. Seeking support: John confides in his partner, close friends, and family members about his stress levels. He seeks their understanding and support, allowing them to provide assistance with childcare, household tasks, or emotional support when needed.

5. Self-care and relaxation: John incorporates regular self-care practices into his routine. He dedicates time each day to activities that help him relax and recharge, such as exercising, practising meditation or mindfulness, reading, or pursuing hobbies. These activities provide a much-needed break from stress and promote emotional well-being.

6. Setting boundaries: John learns to set boundaries at work and communicate his needs to his colleagues and superiors. He establishes clear expectations and delegates tasks when appropriate. By setting boundaries, he creates a healthier work-life balance and reduces stress levels.

7. Seeking professional help: Recognizing the need for additional support, John decides to consult a therapist or counsellor. Through therapy, he learns effective stress management techniques, gains insights into his

coping mechanisms, and develops strategies to navigate the challenges of his high-stress lifestyle.

8. Lifestyle adjustments: John makes lifestyle adjustments to support stress reduction. This includes adopting a healthy diet, getting regular exercise, ensuring sufficient sleep, and avoiding excessive alcohol or caffeine intake. These adjustments provide a solid foundation for managing stress and promoting overall well-being.

Over time, by implementing these strategies, John experiences a noticeable improvement in his stress levels and overall quality of life. He becomes more resilient in dealing with challenges, finds greater fulfilment in his relationships and work, and enjoys a better work-life balance.

John's example illustrates the importance of self-awareness, seeking support, setting boundaries, prioritizing self-care, and making lifestyle adjustments to address and manage stress within a demanding lifestyle.

- **Identifying and Understanding Negative Emotional States**

Negative emotional states are an integral part of human experience. They can arise from various sources, such as personal setbacks, interpersonal conflicts, or external circumstances. It is crucial to identify and understand these negative emotional states to effectively address them and promote emotional well-being. This article explores different types of negative emotions and their impact on individuals and provides examples to facilitate a deeper understanding of these states.

1. Sadness: Sadness is a common negative emotional state characterized by feelings of sorrow, grief, or melancholy. It often arises from loss, disappointment, or unmet expectations. For instance, the loss of a loved one, the end of a significant relationship, or failure to achieve a desired goal can trigger feelings of sadness. Understanding sadness allows individuals to acknowledge their emotions, seek support from others, and engage in self-care activities to cope effectively.

Example: Neeta recently experienced a breakup after a long-term relationship. She feels a profound sense of sadness and loss, often accompanied by tearfulness and a lack of motivation. By recognizing her sadness, Neeta can reach out to friends for emotional support, engage in therapeutic activities like journaling or meditation, and gradually work towards healing.

2. Anger: Anger is an intense emotional state characterized by feelings of hostility, frustration, or rage. It can be triggered by perceived injustices, mistreatment, or an infringement of personal boundaries. Anger, when appropriately managed, can provide energy for positive change. However, uncontrolled anger can lead to destructive behaviours and strained relationships. Understanding the underlying causes of anger is vital for developing healthy coping strategies.

Example: John experiences anger when he feels overlooked or undervalued at work. He notices that his anger often manifests as irritability, a raised voice, and a desire to retaliate. Recognizing his anger allows John to practice self-awareness, adopt relaxation techniques like deep breathing or mindfulness, and communicate assertively to address the root causes of his frustration.

3. Fear: Fear is an emotional response triggered by a perceived threat or danger. It serves as a survival mechanism, preparing individuals to react to potential harm. However, excessive or irrational fear can lead to anxiety disorders and hinder personal growth. Recognizing fear allows individuals to evaluate its validity, challenge distorted thoughts, and gradually confront their fears to regain control.

Example: Emily has a fear of public speaking, which often leads to panic attacks and avoidance behaviours. By identifying her fear, Emily can seek support through therapy or public speaking courses, gradually exposing herself to speaking in front of small groups and desensitizing her fear over time.

4. Guilt: Guilt arises from a sense of responsibility for a perceived wrongdoing. It can stem from violating personal values, hurting others, or failing to meet self-imposed expectations. While guilt can motivate individuals to make amends or improve their behaviour, excessive guilt can lead to self-blame and decreased self-worth. Understanding guilt helps individuals differentiate between healthy remorse and harmful self-punishment.

Example: Michael feels guilty after missing his friend's important event due to work commitments. He acknowledges his guilt, reaches out to his friend to express his remorse, and makes an effort to prioritize personal relationships in the future. By understanding the role of guilt, Michael can learn from his mistakes without letting it consume him.

Conclusion: Identifying and understanding negative emotional states is essential for promoting emotional well-being and personal growth. By recognizing emotions such as sadness, anger, fear, and guilt, individuals can develop effective coping strategies, seek support when needed, and work towards resolving underlying issues. This understanding empowers individuals to navigate through challenging emotions, leading to increased resilience and overall emotional well-being.

- **Anxiety and Stress: Remedies for Inner Calm**

In today's fast-paced world, many people experience anxiety and stress on a regular basis. These feelings can be overwhelming and have a negative impact on our overall well-being. However, there are remedies and practices that can help us find inner calm and reduce anxiety and stress levels. In this article, we will explore some of these remedies and provide examples of how they can be incorporated into our daily lives.

1. Deep Breathing: Deep breathing is a simple yet powerful technique that can quickly calm your mind and body. Start by finding a quiet place where you can sit or lie down comfortably. Close your eyes and take a deep breath in through your nose, allowing your belly to expand. Slowly exhale through your mouth, letting go of any tension or worries. Repeat this process for

a few minutes, focusing on your breath and allowing yourself to relax.

Example: Neeta, a busy executive, often feels overwhelmed by her workload. Whenever she feels her stress levels rising, she takes a few minutes to practice deep breathing. She finds a quiet corner in her office, closes her eyes, and takes several deep breaths. This simple practice helps her feel more centred and reduces her anxiety, allowing her to tackle her tasks with a clearer mind.

2. Mindfulness Meditation: Mindfulness meditation involves focusing your attention on the present moment without judgment. It helps bring awareness to your thoughts and feelings, allowing you to observe them without getting caught up in them. Regular practice of mindfulness meditation can increase self-awareness and reduce anxiety and stress.

Example: Mark, a college student, often finds it difficult to concentrate on his studies due to anxiety. He decided to incorporate mindfulness meditation into his daily routine. Each morning, he sets aside 10 minutes to sit quietly and focus on his breath. Whenever his mind wanders, he gently brings his attention back to the present moment. Over time, Mark noticed a significant reduction in his anxiety levels, and he is better able to stay focused on his studies.

3. Exercise: Engaging in regular physical activity is not only beneficial for your physical health but also your mental well-being. Exercise releases endorphins, which are natural mood-boosting chemicals in the brain. It

can help reduce anxiety and stress levels and improve overall mood.

Example: Lisa, a working professional, often feels stressed after a long day at the office. Instead of turning to unhealthy coping mechanisms, she decides to incorporate exercise into her routine. She joins a local yoga class and attends sessions three times a week. Not only does the physical activity help her release tension from her body, but the mindfulness aspect of yoga also helps her find inner calm and tranquillity.

4. Journaling: Writing down your thoughts and feelings in a journal can be a therapeutic practice. It allows you to release emotions, gain clarity, and process stressful events. Journaling can be done in various forms, such as free writing, gratitude journaling, or reflective writing.

Example: John, a freelancer, often experiences anxiety about his financial situation. To help manage his stress, he started journaling regularly. Each evening, he spends 10 minutes reflecting on his day and writing down any thoughts or concerns that come to mind. Through this practice, John realizes that many of his worries are unfounded, and he begins to focus on the positive aspects of his life. Journaling becomes a valuable tool for him to find inner calm and cultivate gratitude.

5. Time in Nature: Spending time in nature has been shown to reduce stress and anxiety levels. Being surrounded by natural environments can have a calming effect on the mind and body. Whether it's taking a walk in the park, hiking in the mountains, or simply sitting by a

lake, connecting with nature can help restore a sense of inner peace.

Example: Emma, a busy parent, often feels overwhelmed by her responsibilities. She decides to make time for nature walks with her family on weekends. They explore nearby hiking trails and spend quality time together in nature. Emma notices that being surrounded by the beauty of the outdoors helps her let go of stress and find a sense of calm. Nature walks become a cherished activity that brings tranquillity to her and her family.

In conclusion, anxiety and stress are common challenges in today's society, but there are remedies that can help us find inner calm. Deep breathing, mindfulness meditation, regular exercise, journaling, and spending time in nature are just a few examples of practices that can reduce anxiety and stress levels. By incorporating these remedies into our daily lives, we can cultivate a greater sense of peace and well-being. Remember, finding inner calm is a journey, and it may take time to discover what works best for you.

- **Fear and Phobias: Overcoming Emotional Barriers**

Fear and phobias are powerful emotions that can create significant barriers in our lives. They can hold us back from pursuing our goals, engaging in social interactions, or even enjoying everyday activities. Overcoming these emotional barriers is crucial for personal growth and overall well-being. In this response, I will discuss the process of overcoming fear and phobias and provide an example to illustrate these concepts.

1. Recognizing the fear or phobia: The first step in overcoming any emotional barrier is to identify and acknowledge its presence. This requires self-reflection and an honest assessment of your feelings. Take the time to understand the specific fear or phobia you're facing, whether it's fear of heights, spiders, public speaking, or any other situation that triggers intense anxiety.

2. Understanding the root cause: Once you've identified your fear or phobia, it's essential to explore its origins. Often, fears and phobias stem from past traumatic experiences, learned behaviour, or even irrational thought patterns. Understanding the root cause can help you gain perspective and challenge the underlying beliefs that reinforce your fear.

3. Seeking professional help: Overcoming deep-rooted fears and phobias can be challenging on your own. Consider seeking professional help, such as therapy or counselling. Mental health professionals are trained to guide you through the process and provide you with the necessary tools and techniques to manage and overcome your fears effectively.

4. Gradual exposure and desensitization: One of the most effective ways to conquer fears and phobias is through gradual exposure and desensitization. This involves facing your fear in a controlled and safe environment, starting with less challenging situations and gradually

progressing to more anxiety-provoking ones. For instance, if you have a fear of flying, you might start by watching videos of aeroplanes, then visiting an airport, and eventually taking a short flight.

5. Cognitive-behavioral techniques: Cognitive-behavioral therapy (CBT) techniques can be particularly helpful in overcoming fears and phobias. CBT focuses on identifying and challenging negative thought patterns and replacing them with more realistic and positive ones. This process helps ref Neeta e your perception of the feared situation and reduces the associated anxiety.

Example: Let's consider an example of someone named Neeta who has a fear of public speaking. Neeta's fear prevents her from pursuing career opportunities and sharing her ideas effectively in professional settings. Recognizing the impact of her fear, she decides to overcome it.

Neeta begins by acknowledging her fear and understanding that it stems from a past embarrassing experience during a school presentation. With the help of a therapist, Neeta explores the root cause and realizes that her fear is based on irrational thoughts of judgment and humiliation.

To address her fear, Neeta engages in gradual exposure and desensitization. She starts by practising her presentation skills in front of a mirror, then with a trusted friend or family member, and eventually in front of small groups of people. With each successful experience, her confidence and comfort levels increase.

Simultaneously, Neeta learns cognitive-behavioural techniques to challenge her negative thoughts. She replaces self-defeating beliefs with positive affirmations, reminding herself that everyone makes mistakes and that her worth is not solely determined by her performance in public speaking.

Over time, Neeta's fear of public speaking diminishes significantly. She feels more confident and capable of expressing herself in professional settings, which opens doors for career advancement and greater personal growth.

In conclusion, overcoming fear and phobias requires self-awareness, understanding the root cause, seeking professional help when needed, gradual exposure, and the application of cognitive-behavioural techniques. By actively confronting our fears, we can break through emotional barriers and lead more fulfilling lives.

- **Sadness and Grief: Restoring Emotional Balance**

Sadness and grief are universal human emotions that we all experience at some point in our lives. Whether it's the loss of a loved one, the end of a relationship, or any significant life change, these emotions can feel overwhelming and disrupt our emotional balance. However, it's crucial to acknowledge that these emotions are a natural part of the human experience. Chapter, we will explore strategies and examples of how to navigate sadness and grief, restore emotional balance, and find solace amidst challenging times.

Body:

1. Recognizing and Accepting Sadness and Grief: The first step towards restoring emotional balance is to acknowledge and accept the presence of sadness and grief in our lives. It's important to give ourselves permission to feel these emotions without judgment or resistance. By recognizing the validity of our emotions, we can begin the healing process.

Example: After the sudden loss of her beloved pet dog, Neeta found herself engulfed in overwhelming sadness. Instead of suppressing her emotions, she allowed herself to grieve fully. Neeta acknowledged her pain and created a memorial space in her home where she could honour her dog's memory. By accepting her sadness, she opened the door to healing and restoring her emotional balance.

2. Seeking Support and Connection: During times of sadness and grief, it's crucial to reach out for support and connect with others. Sharing our feelings with trusted friends family members, or even seeking professional help can provide solace and comfort. Human connection plays a vital role in restoring emotional balance.

Example: After the end of a long-term relationship, Michael felt a deep sense of loss and isolation. Recognizing the need for support, he reached out to a therapist who specialized in grief counselling. Through therapy, he was able to process his emotions, gain perspective, and find a renewed sense of hope. Additionally, he joined a support group where he could connect with others experiencing similar emotions, fostering a sense of community and emotional balance.

3. Engaging in Self-Care Practices: Taking care of ourselves physically, emotionally, and mentally is essential in restoring emotional balance during times of sadness and grief. Engaging in self-care practices helps us nourish our well-being and find moments of respite amidst the storm of emotions.

Example: Laura, a single mother, found herself overwhelmed with grief after the passing of her mother. In order to restore emotional balance, she prioritized self-care by incorporating activities she loved into her daily routine. She began journaling to process her emotions, started practising yoga for relaxation, and made sure to spend quality time with her children and friends. By dedicating time to herself and engaging in activities that brought her joy, Laura gradually found solace and emotional equilibrium.

Conclusion: Sadness and grief are natural responses to life's challenges, but they need not define us indefinitely. By recognizing and accepting these emotions, seeking support, and engaging in self-care practices, we can restore emotional balance and find moments of peace and healing. Remember, healing takes time, and each individual's journey is unique. By practising patience, compassion, and self-care, we can navigate through sadness and grief, emerging stronger and more resilient on the other side.

- **Lack of Confidence and Self-Esteem: Empowering the Self**

Confidence and self-esteem are essential ingredients for personal growth and success. They enable individuals to face challenges, pursue their goals, and overcome obstacles with resilience. However, many people struggle with a lack of confidence and low self-esteem, which can hinder their progress and limit their potential. In this essay, we will explore the concept of self-empowerment as a means to overcome these challenges. By understanding and implementing empowering strategies, individuals can transform their self-perception, boost their confidence, and build a solid foundation of self-esteem.

Body:

1. Understanding the Roots of Low Confidence and Self-Esteem: Low confidence and self-esteem often have deep-rooted causes. It can stem from childhood experiences, negative self-talk, societal pressures, or a combination of these factors. Understanding the origins of these issues is the first step towards empowering oneself. By recognizing the sources, individuals can address them more effectively and break free from their negative impact.

2. Challenging Negative Self-Talk and Limiting Beliefs: Negative self-talk and limiting beliefs are significant contributors to low confidence and self-esteem. The inner dialogue we have with ourselves can shape our perceptions and actions. To empower oneself, it is crucial to identify and challenge these negative thoughts. By replacing them with positive affirmations and refNeeta ing perspectives, individuals can gradually

shift their mindset and build a more positive self-image.

3. Setting Realistic Goals and Celebrating Progress: Setting realistic goals and celebrating small achievements play a vital role in building confidence and self-esteem. By breaking down larger goals into smaller, manageable steps, individuals can experience a sense of accomplishment along the way. Celebrating these milestones, no matter how small reinforces the belief in one's abilities and fuels motivation for further progress.

4. Embracing Failure as a Stepping Stone: Fear of failure often holds people back from pursuing their dreams and reaching their full potential. However, failure is an inevitable part of growth and learning. Embracing failure as a stepping stone to success is an empowering mindset. By referring to failures as valuable lessons, individuals can overcome setbacks, learn from their mistakes, and grow stronger in the process. This perspective shift fosters resilience and cultivates a growth-oriented mindset.

5. Cultivating Self-Care and Healthy Boundaries: Self-empowerment involves taking care of oneself holistically. Prioritizing self-care, including physical, emotional, and mental well-being, is essential to boost confidence and self-esteem. Engaging in activities that promote self-reflection, relaxation, and personal growth nurtures a positive self-image. Additionally,

establishing healthy boundaries in relationships and knowing one's worth contributes to a sense of self-respect and empowerment.

Overcoming a lack of confidence and low self-esteem is a transformative journey that requires dedication and self-reflection. Through self-empowerment, individuals can break free from the limitations imposed by their negative self-perceptions. By understanding the roots of their issues, challenging negative self-talk, setting realistic goals, embracing failure, and practising self-care, individuals can build a strong foundation of confidence and self-esteem. Empowering oneself is a continuous process that requires perseverance, but the rewards are immense. With increased confidence and self-esteem, individuals can navigate life's challenges, pursue their aspirations, and lead a more fulfilling and purposeful existence.

Chapter : 4

Exploring the Bach Flower Remedies

*All we have to do is preserve our personality, live our own life,
be captain of our own ship, and all will be well.*
- EDWARD BACH

In the context of Bach Flower Remedies, this statement reinforces the idea that emotional well-being and harmony come from aligning with one's true self and embracing one's unique personality. The remedies are designed to support individuals in reconnecting with their authentic nature and finding inner balance.

By acknowledging and addressing emotional imbalances, individuals can become better captains of their own ships, navigating the seas of life with greater clarity, resilience, and inner peace. The remedies serve as tools to help individuals preserve and enhance their personalities while finding greater harmony within themselves.

Bach Flower Remedies are a system of natural remedies developed by Dr. Edward Bach in the 1930s. Dr. Bach believed that emotional imbalances and negative emotions were the root causes of physical illnesses and sought to address these imbalances through flower essences. The remedies are made from the essences of specific flowers and are believed to have a balancing effect on emotions.

There are 38 different Bach Flower Remedies, each corresponding to a specific emotional state or personality trait. Some of the most commonly used remedies include:

1. Rescue Remedy: This is a combination of five Bach Flower Remedies (Rock Rose, Impatiens, Clematis, Star of Bethlehem, and Cherry Plum) and is used for acute stress and emergencies. It is often used to promote a sense of calm and stability.

2. Mimulus: This remedy is used for known fears and specific anxieties, such as fear of flying, fear of public speaking, or fear of spiders.

3. Rock Rose: This remedy is used for extreme fear or panic, such as during a traumatic event or a sudden intense fear.

4. Walnut: This remedy is used during periods of change or transition, helping individuals adjust and adapt to new circumstances.

5. Gentian: This remedy is used for feelings of discouragement, despondency, and scepticism.

6. Olive: This remedy is used for exhaustion, both physical and mental. It is often used to restore vitality and energy.

These are just a few examples, and each of the 38 remedies is believed to address a specific emotional state or imbalance. The remedies are typically taken orally in the form of liquid drops, although they can also be applied topically or added to bathwater.

It's important to note that Bach Flower Remedies are considered complementary or alternative remedies and are not intended to replace medical treatment for physical or mental health conditions. If you have a serious or chronic health issue, it's important to consult with a qualified healthcare professional.

Some people find Bach Flower Remedies to be helpful in addressing emotional imbalances and promoting overall well-being, while others may not experience significant effects. As with any natural remedy, individual experiences may vary.

- **Chapter dedicated to each of the 38 remedies**

Bach Flower Remedies, developed by Dr. Edward Bach in the 1930s, offer a natural and holistic approach to emotional well-being. These remedies are derived from the essences of different flowers and plants, each thought to address specific emotional imbalances. In this book, we embark on a transformative journey, dedicating a chapter to each of the 38 remedies. Through this exploration, we aim to gain a deeper understanding of their unique healing properties and their potential to restore harmony within.

1. Agrimony:

    - Indications: Inner conflict, emotional masks, avoidance of confrontation

    - Healing properties: Encourages authenticity, emotional honesty, and self-acceptance

2. Aspen:

    - Indications: Unexplained anxieties, fear of the unknown

- Healing properties: Instils peace, trust, and inner guidance

3. Beech:

- Indications: Intolerance, critical attitude, judgmental behaviour
- Healing properties: Fosters empathy, understanding, and acceptance

4. Centaury:

- Indications: Submissiveness, difficulty saying no, people-pleasing
- Healing properties: Empowers individuals, fosters assertiveness and self-care

5. Cerato:

- Indications: Self-doubt, indecisiveness, seeking external validation
- Healing properties: Enhances intuition, self-trust, and inner wisdom

6. Cherry Plum:

- Indications: Fear of losing control, fear of the mind "snapping"
- Healing properties: Restores emotional equilibrium and inner stability

7. Chestnut Bud:

- Indications: Difficulty learning from past experiences, repeating mistakes

- Healing properties: Promotes observation, reflection, and personal growth

8. Chicory:

- Indications: Overly possessive, manipulative, seeking attention

- Healing properties: Cultivates selflessness, unconditional love, and healthy boundaries

9. Clematis:

- Indications: Daydreaming, lack of focus, escapism

- Healing properties: Enhances mental clarity, presence, and groundedness

10. Crab Apple:

- Indications: Self-consciousness, feeling unclean, body image issues

- Healing properties: Supports self-acceptance, purification, and renewal

11. Elm:

- Indications: Overwhelm from responsibilities, temporary self-doubt

- Healing properties: Restores confidence, resilience, and perspective

12. Gentian:

- Indications: Discouragement, despondency, setbacks

- Healing properties: Instils faith, optimism, and perseverance

13. Gorse:

- Indications: Hopelessness, despair, giving up
- Healing properties: Cultivates hope, inner strength, and renewed faith

14. Heather:

- Indications: Self-centeredness, excessive talking, need for company
- Healing properties: Fosters empathy, listening skills, and inner peace

15. Holly:

- Indications: Anger, envy, jealousy, suspicion
- Healing properties: Promotes love, compassion, and emotional balance

16. Honeysuckle:

- Indications: Living in the past, nostalgia, homesickness
- Healing properties: Supports living in the present, embracing change, and letting go

17. Hornbeam:

- Indications: Mental fatigue, procrastination, lack of enthusiasm

- Healing properties: Restores mental vitality, motivation, and zest for life

18. Impatiens:

- Indications: Impatience, irritability, tension

- Healing properties: Cultivates patience, inner calm, and understanding

19. Larch:

- Indications: Lack of confidence, self-doubt, fear of failure

- Healing properties: Boosts self-esteem, self-assurance, and courage

20. Mimulus:

- Indications: Known fears, phobias, timidity

- Healing properties: Instils courage, confidence, and inner strength

21. Mustard:

- Indications: Deep sadness, gloominess without apparent cause

- Healing properties: Restores joy, inner light, and emotional stability

22. Oak:

- Indications: Perseverance, despite exhaustion or overwork

- Healing properties: Balances effort with rest, restores resilience and flexibility

23. Olive:

- Indications: Physical and mental exhaustion, lack of vitality

- Healing properties: Revitalizes energy, restores strength, and rejuvenates the spirit

24. Pine:

- Indications: Guilt, self-blame, feelings of unworthiness

- Healing properties: Encourages self-forgiveness, self-acceptance, and inner peace

25. Red Chestnut:

- Indications: Excessive worry and fear for the well-being of others

- Healing properties: Cultivates trust, healthy concern, and emotional balance

26. Rock Rose:

- Indications: Intense fear, panic, terror

- Healing properties: Restores courage, calmness, and inner strength in the face of fear

27. Rock Water:

- Indications: Perfectionism, rigid self-discipline, self-denial

- Healing properties: Promotes flexibility, self-acceptance, and inner balance

28. Scleranthus:

- Indications: Indecisiveness, fluctuating moods, inner imbalance

- Healing properties: Fosters balance, decisiveness, and emotional stability

29. Star of Bethlehem:

- Indications: Trauma, shock, emotional wounds

- Healing properties: Supports healing, comfort, and emotional recovery

30. Sweet Chestnut:

- Indications: Extreme mental anguish, despair, feeling at the limits of endurance

- Healing properties: Brings solace, strength, and a renewed sense of hope

31. Vervain:

- Indications: Overenthusiasm, overwork, tension

- Healing properties: Promotes relaxation, balance, and a more moderate approach

32. Vine:

- Indications: Dominance, inflexibility, authority-seeking

- Healing properties: Encourages leadership, assertiveness, and consideration for others

33. Walnut:

- Indications: Difficulty adapting to change, sensitivity to outside influences

- Healing properties: Supports transitions, protection, and personal boundaries

34. Water Violet:

- Indications: Aloofness, pride, a desire for solitude

- Healing properties: Fosters connection, openness, and a sense of community

35. White Chestnut:

- Indications: Persistent unwanted thoughts, mental chatter

- Healing properties: Calms the mind, promotes clarity, and inner peace

36. Wild Oat:

- Indications: Uncertainty about life path, feeling unfulfilled

- Healing properties: Helps find direction, purpose, and clarity of life's calling

37. Wild Rose:

- Indications: Resignation, apathy, lack of motivation

- Healing properties: Restores enthusiasm, interest, and zest for life

38. Willow:

- Indications: Resentment, bitterness, feeling victimized

- Healing properties: Cultivates forgiveness, resilience, and emotional liberation

Each of these remedies carries its own unique qualities and can be used to address specific emotional imbalances. Remember, it's important to consult a qualified practitioner or conduct further research to determine the most suitable remedy for individual needs.

- **Properties, Indications, and Benefits**

Bach Flower Remedies offer a unique approach to emotional healing and well-being. Derived from the essences of various flowers and plants, these remedies are known for their gentle yet powerful effects on emotional imbalances. Here, we explore the properties, indications, and benefits of Bach Flower Remedies, highlighting their versatility and potential in promoting emotional harmony.

1. Properties of Bach Flower Remedies:

- Natural: Bach Flower Remedies are made from natural sources, primarily flowers and plants, making them safe for use and free from harmful side effects.

- Vibrational: These remedies work on an energetic level, addressing the underlying emotional imbalances that contribute to physical and mental well-being.

- Holistic: Bach Flower Remedies aim to treat the individual as a whole, considering emotional, mental, and spiritual aspects of well-being.

2. Indications and Benefits:

- Anxiety and Fear: Remedies like Aspen, Mimulus, and Rock Rose are indicated for different types of fear, ranging from known fears to unexplained anxieties and extreme panic.

- Uncertainty and Indecision: Remedies like Scleranthus and Cerato are beneficial for individuals who struggle with decision-making, lack clarity, or seek external validation.

- Overwhelm and Despair: Remedies such as Elm, Sweet Chestnut, and Gorse address emotional states characterized by overwhelming responsibilities, deep sadness, or feelings of hopelessness.

- Lack of Motivation and Interest: Remedies like Wild Rose and Hornbeam are indicated for individuals who feel apathetic, lack enthusiasm, or struggle to find joy and purpose in life.

- Self-Doubt and Self-Confidence: Remedies such as Larch and Cerato can help individuals boost self-confidence, overcome self-doubt, and trust their own abilities and intuition.

- Emotional Healing and Support: Remedies like Star of Bethlehem and Walnut offer support during times of emotional trauma, major life transitions, or when dealing with external influences.

3.   Individualized Approach:

- One of the key principles of Bach Flower Remedies is the individualized approach. Each remedy is selected based on the specific emotional state and personality traits of the person, tailoring the treatment to their unique needs.

- It is important to consult with a qualified Bach Flower Practitioner or a trained professional who can assess and determine the most suitable remedies for an individual's emotional well-being.

4.   Complementary Nature:

- Bach Flower Remedies are complementary in nature, meaning they can be used alongside other conventional or alternative therapies without interfering with their effects.

- They can be used by individuals of all ages, including children, pregnant women, and the elderly.

5. Self-Care and Prevention:

- Bach Flower Remedies can be used as part of a proactive self-care routine to maintain emotional balance, prevent emotional imbalances from escalating, and promote overall well-being.

- Regular use of Bach Flower Remedies can help individuals become more attuned to their emotions, develop self-awareness, and foster a greater sense of emotional resilience.

Conclusion: Bach Flower Remedies possess unique properties that make them an effective and versatile tool for addressing emotional imbalances. Indicated for a wide range of emotional states and offering individualized support, these remedies can bring about profound benefits, including reduced anxiety, increased self-confidence, and enhanced emotional well-being. As a complementary approach to emotional healing, Bach Flower Remedies provide a holistic pathway to restoring emotional balance and promoting overall wellness.

- **Case Studies and Testimonials**

Case Studies and Testimonials: Harnessing the Healing Power of Bach Flower Remedies

Introduction: Bach Flower Remedies have garnered significant recognition for their ability to address emotional imbalances and promote overall well-being. Through the use of flower essences, these remedies offer a gentle and natural approach to emotional healing. In this chapter, we will delve into a collection of case studies and testimonials, showcasing the transformative effects of Bach Flower Remedies in real-life situations. By examining these stories of personal growth and healing, we aim to highlight the power and versatility of Bach Flower Remedies as a complementary therapy for emotional well-being.

Case Study 1: Overcoming Social Anxiety with Mimulus Mary, a 32-year-old woman, had been struggling with debilitating social anxiety for years. She found it challenging to engage in social situations, often experiencing intense fear and a racing heart. After consulting with a Bach Flower Practitioner, Mary started taking Mimulus, a remedy specifically designed to address known fears and phobias. Over time, Mary noticed a significant improvement in her ability to cope with social situations. She became more confident, gradually pushing herself outside of her comfort zone. Through the gentle support of Mimulus, Mary overcame her social anxiety and was able to enjoy a fulfilling social life once again.

Case Study 2: Restoring Inner Peace with Rock Rose-John, a combat veteran, suffered from recurring nightmares and severe anxiety as a result of his traumatic experiences in the military. Seeking relief, he turned to Bach Flower Remedies and began taking Rock Rose, known for its ability to address extreme fear and panic. With consistent use, John experienced a remarkable reduction in his nightmares and a newfound sense of inner peace. Rock Rose empowered him to confront his fears head-on and regain control over his emotional well-being. This case study demonstrates the profound impact Bach Flower Remedies can have on individuals dealing with trauma-related anxiety and fear.

Testimonial 1: Rediscovering Joy with Wild Rose - Emily, a middle-aged woman, had been feeling stuck in a rut, lacking motivation or interest in life. She described a persistent feeling of apathy and emotional numbness. Upon consultation with a Bach Flower Practitioner, Emily began taking Wild Rose, a remedy that rekindles enthusiasm and restores zest for life. Within a few weeks, Emily noticed a significant shift in her perspective. She became more engaged in her hobbies, started pursuing new interests, and rediscovered a sense of joy and purpose. The testimonial of Emily emphasizes the transformative potential of Bach Flower Remedies in revitalizing one's emotional state and restoring a vibrant outlook on life.

Testimonial 2: Finding Inner Clarity with Cerato -Neeta, a young professional, struggled with indecisiveness and constant self-doubt. She often sought external validation and had difficulty trusting her own judgment. Upon recommendation, Neeta began taking Cerato, a remedy that encourages inner guidance and self-trust. As she continued her journey with Cerato, Neeta noticed a remarkable improvement in her decision-making process. She became more confident in trusting her intuition and found clarity in various aspects of her life, including career choices and personal relationships. Neeta's testimonial underscores the empowering effects of Bach Flower Remedies in fostering self-confidence and cultivating inner wisdom.

The case studies and testimonials presented in this chapter provide compelling evidence of the transformative power of Bach Flower Remedies. From overcoming social anxiety and trauma-related fear to rediscovering joy and finding inner clarity, these stories demonstrate the profound impact of flower essences on emotional well-being. By harnessing the healing potential of Bach Flower Remedies, individuals can embark on a journey of personal growth, self-discovery, and emotional balance. These accounts serve as a testament to the effectiveness and versatility of Bach Flower Remedies as a valuable tool in supporting emotional health and well-being.

Choosing and Using Bach Flower Remedies

Every single person has a life to live, a work to do, a glorious personality, a wonderful individuality.
- Edward Bach

When selecting and using Bach Flower Remedies, it's essential to recognize and honour the uniqueness of each individual. Just as Dr. Bach believed that every person possesses a glorious personality and a wonderful individuality, the remedies are designed to address the specific emotional and mental needs of each person.

Choosing the right Bach Flower Remedies involves a thoughtful consideration of an individual's emotional state, personality traits, and emotional imbalances. It acknowledges that each person's journey toward emotional well-being is unique and deeply personal.

Furthermore, using Bach Flower Remedies with this perspective encourages individuals to embrace their individuality and recognize the inherent worth within themselves. The remedies serve as a means to support and enhance one's authentic self, fostering greater emotional balance and inner harmony in the process.

Bach Flower Remedies are a natural and gentle form of healing that can help balance emotional and mental well-being. Developed by Dr. Edward Bach in the early 20th century, these remedies are based on the belief that emotional imbalances can contribute to physical illnesses. Bach Flower Remedies aim to address these emotional imbalances and promote overall health. In this guide, we will explore how to choose and use Bach Flower Remedies effectively to enhance your emotional and mental wellness.

Understanding Bach Flower Remedies

Bach Flower Remedies consist of 38 different flower essences, each targeting specific emotional states or personality traits. These essences are prepared by infusing flowers in spring water and preserving them with a small amount of brandy. They are completely safe and free from side effects, making them suitable for people of all ages, including children and pets.

Choosing the Right Remedy

Selecting the right Bach Flower Remedy begins with self-awareness. Take the time to reflect on your emotional state and identify the specific feelings or behaviours you want to address. Once you have a clear understanding of your emotions, you can choose the remedy that resonates with your current situation. Here are some common Bach Flower Remedies and the emotions they address:

1. **Rescue Remedy (Five-Flower Formula):** This is a combination remedy that can be used for general stress and anxiety, as well as in times of crisis.

2. **Agrimony:** For those who hide their worries behind a cheerful facade.

3.   **Impatiens:** For impatient individuals who are easily irritated.

4.   **Mimulus:** To address specific fears and phobias, such as fear of the dark or fear of public speaking.

5.   **Cherry Plum:** For those who fear losing control of their emotions or actions.

6.   **White Chestnut:** To quiet the mind and ease repetitive, worrisome thoughts.

7.   **Rock Rose:** For extreme fear and panic, often associated with traumatic events.

8.   **Gentian:** To boost confidence and overcome discouragement from setbacks.

9.   **Star of Bethlehem:** For emotional trauma, shock, or grief.

Using Bach Flower Remedies

Once you've chosen the appropriate Bach Flower Remedy, it's essential to use it correctly:

1.   **Dilution:** Bach Flower Remedies are highly concentrated, so they should be diluted before use. Add two drops of the chosen remedy to a glass of water and sip it throughout the day.

2.   **Frequency:** Take the diluted remedy at least four times a day, ideally more frequently if needed. The goal is to maintain a consistent presence of the remedy in your system.

3. **Duration:** Continue taking the remedy until you notice a positive change in your emotional state. This may vary from a few days to several weeks, depending on the individual and the issue being addressed.

4. **Combining Remedies:** If you find that multiple emotional issues are affecting you, you can combine up to seven Bach Flower Remedies to create a personalized blend.

5. **Observation:** Pay close attention to any changes in your emotional state, as well as any physical improvements. Keep a journal to track your progress.

6. **Rescue Remedy**: In times of acute stress or crisis, you can take Rescue Remedy directly by placing four drops under your tongue or adding it to a glass of water.

Bach Flower Remedies offer a natural and non-invasive approach to emotional well-being. By choosing the right remedy and using it as directed, you can address emotional imbalances and support your overall health and vitality. Remember that Bach Flower Remedies are not a substitute for professional medical care, so if you have severe or persistent emotional issues, it's essential to consult with a healthcare provider or therapist. Nevertheless, for many, these remedies provide a valuable tool for finding emotional balance and harmony in daily life.

- **Selecting the Right Remedy for Specific Emotional States**

Before delving into the individual remedies, it's essential to understand the philosophy behind Bach Flower Remedies. Dr.

Bach believed that negative emotions and attitudes could lead to physical illnesses. To counteract these emotional imbalances, he developed a system of 38 flower essences, each addressing a particular emotional state or personality trait. These remedies are prepared by infusing the essence of specific flowers in spring water and preserving them with a small amount of brandy.

Choosing the right Bach Flower Remedy begins with introspection and self-awareness. You need to identify the emotions or behaviours you want to address. Once you have a clear understanding of your emotional state, you can select the appropriate remedy that resonates with your feelings and needs.

Common Bach Flower Remedies and Their Emotional States

1. **Agrimony:** This remedy is for individuals who hide their inner turmoil behind a cheerful facade. They may be suffering from deep-seated anxieties or worries but prefer to keep them hidden. Agrimony helps individuals confront and address their inner conflicts.

2. **Aspen:** For vague and unexplained fears, anxiety, and apprehension. This remedy is beneficial for those who are prone to anxiety attacks or have a sense of impending doom without a clear cause.

3. **Beech:** Beech is for those who are overly critical, intolerant, and judgmental. It helps individuals cultivate greater tolerance and acceptance of others.

4. **Centaury:** People who find it challenging to say no and often overextend themselves benefit from Centaury.

This remedy empowers individuals to assert themselves without feeling overwhelmed.

5. **Cerato:** For individuals who constantly seek advice and validation from others and struggle to trust their intuition and judgment. Cerato helps individuals regain confidence in their decision-making abilities.

6. **Cherry Plum:** This remedy is for those who fear losing control of their emotions or actions, especially during moments of extreme stress or anger.

7. **Chestnut Bud:** For those who repeatedly make the same mistakes or fail to learn from past experiences. Chestnut Bud encourages awareness and the ability to break destructive patterns.

8. **Chicory:** Chicory is for individuals who are possessive, manipulative, and overly controlling in their relationships. It helps promote more selfless and unconditional love.

9. **Clematis:** For individuals who are dreamy, absent-minded, and disconnected from the present. Clematis promotes a sense of groundedness and helps individuals manifest their dreams in reality.

10. **Crab Apple:** This remedy is for those who are excessively self-conscious and obsessed with cleanliness and order. Crab Apple helps individuals accept themselves and their imperfections.

11. **Elm:** Elm is for individuals who feel overwhelmed by

responsibilities and tasks. It helps restore confidence and the ability to handle life's challenges.

12. **Gentian:** For individuals who easily become discouraged by setbacks and challenges. Gentian promotes resilience and the ability to stay positive in the face of adversity.

13. **Gorse**: Gorse is for those who have lost hope and feel despair. It helps individuals find renewed faith and optimism in life.

14. **Heather:** This remedy is for individuals who are excessively self-absorbed and constantly seek attention and validation from others. Heather promotes greater empathy and the ability to listen to others.

15. **Holly:** For individuals who struggle with jealousy, hatred, and suspicion. Holly helps open the heart to love and compassion.

16. **Honeysuckle:** Honeysuckle is for those who dwell on the past and find it challenging to move forward in life. It helps individuals let go of the past and embrace the present.

17. **Hornbeam:** For individuals who feel tired and mentally fatigued, especially when facing monotonous or routine tasks. Hornbeam restores mental vitality and enthusiasm.

18. **Impatiens:** This remedy is for impatient individuals who are easily irritated by the slowness of others. It

helps individuals cultivate patience and tolerance.

19. **Larch:** For those who lack confidence and doubt their abilities. Larch promotes self-assuredness and a belief in one's potential.

20. **Mimulus:** This remedy is for specific fears and phobias, such as fear of the dark, fear of heights, or fear of public speaking. Mimulus helps individuals face and overcome their fears.

21. **Mustard:** Mustard is for individuals who experience deep and unexplained gloom or depression that descends like a dark cloud. It helps dispel these feelings and restore a sense of inner light.

22. **Oak:** For those who are dedicated and hardworking but tend to overexert themselves. Oak helps individuals find balance and the ability to rest when needed.

23. **Olive:** This remedy is for extreme physical and mental exhaustion. Olive helps restore vitality and energy.

24. **Pine:** For individuals who feel guilty and self-blame, even when they are not at fault. Pine promotes self-forgiveness and self-acceptance.

25. **Red Chestnut:** Red Chestnut is for individuals who are excessively worried about the well-being of others, often to the point of anxiety. It helps individuals maintain healthy boundaries and trust in others' abilities to care for themselves.

26. **Rock Rose:** For extreme fear and panic, often associated with traumatic events. Rock Rose provides courage and the ability to face life's challenges.

27. **Rock Water:** This remedy is for individuals who are rigid, perfectionistic, and overly self-disciplined. Rock Water helps individuals find greater flexibility and self-acceptance.

28. **Scleranthus:** For individuals who struggle with indecision and fluctuate between choices. Scleranthus promotes inner balance and decisiveness.

29. **Star of Bethlehem:** For emotional trauma, shock, or grief, whether recent or from the past. The Star of Bethlehem provides comfort and healing.

30. **Sweet Chestnut:** This remedy is for individuals who experience extreme mental anguish and despair, often feeling like they've reached the limits of their endurance. Sweet Chestnut offers hope and the strength to persevere.

31. **Vervain:** For those who are highly strung, intense, and passionate about their beliefs. Vervain helps individuals relax and find a more balanced approach to life.

32. **Vine:** This remedy is for individuals who are domineering and inflexible in their behaviour, often seeking to control others. Vine promotes more assertive yet considerate leadership.

33. **Walnut:** For individuals experiencing significant

life changes and transitions or those who are easily influenced by others. Walnut helps protect against external influences and supports personal growth.

34. **Water Violet:** This remedy is for individuals who prefer solitude and find it challenging to connect with others emotionally. Water Violet helps individuals open up and form meaningful relationships.

35. **White Chestnut:** To quiet the mind and ease repetitive, worrisome thoughts. White Chestnut promotes mental clarity and inner peace.

36. **Wild Oat:** For those who feel directionless and uncertain about their life's purpose. Wild Oat helps individuals find their true calling and path in life.

37. **Wild Rose:** For individuals who have resigned themselves to an unfulfilling and joyless life. Wild Rose restores enthusiasm and a sense of purpose.

38. **Willow:** For individuals who harbour resentment, bitterness, and a sense of unfairness. Willow helps individuals let go of negative emotions and find forgiveness.

Selecting the Right Remedy

To choose the right Bach Flower Remedy for your specific emotional state, follow these steps:

1. **Self-Reflection:** Take the time to introspect and identify the emotions or behaviours you want to

address. Be honest with yourself about your feelings and experiences.

2. **Consult Resources:** Utilize books, online resources, or Bach Flower practitioners to learn more about each remedy's indications. You can also consider consulting with a Bach Flower therapist for personalized guidance.

3. **Trust Your Intuition:** Sometimes, a remedy may resonate with you on an intuitive level. Trust your gut feeling when selecting a remedy.

4. **Consider Combinations:** If you find that multiple emotional issues are affecting you, you can combine up to seven Bach Flower Remedies to create a personalized blend.

5. **Start with One Remedy:** Begin with a single remedy that best matches your primary emotional state. Bach Flower Remedies are gentle, and starting with one allows you to observe its effects.

Using Bach Flower Remedies

Once you've selected the appropriate Bach Flower Remedy, it's essential to use it correctly:

1. **Dilution:** Bach Flower Remedies are highly concentrated, so they should be diluted before use. Add two drops of the chosen remedy to a glass of water and sip it throughout the day.

2. **Frequency:** Take the diluted remedy at least four times

a day, ideally more frequently if needed. The goal is to maintain a consistent presence of the remedy in your system.

3. **Duration:** Continue taking the remedy until you notice a positive change in your emotional state. This may vary from a few days to several weeks, depending on the individual and the issue being addressed.

4. **Combining Remedies:** If you're using a combination of remedies, follow the same dilution and frequency guidelines for each remedy in the blend.

5. **Observation:** Pay close attention to any changes in your emotional state, as well as any physical improvements. Keep a journal to track your progress.

6. **Rescue Remedy:** In times of acute stress or crisis, you can take Rescue Remedy directly by placing four drops under your tongue or adding it to a glass of water.

Bach Flower Remedies offer a gentle and natural way to address specific emotional states and promote emotional well-being. By understanding the emotional indications of each remedy and selecting the one that aligns with your feelings and needs, you can embark on a journey of self-discovery and healing. Remember that Bach Flower Remedies are not a substitute for professional medical care, so if you have severe or persistent emotional issues, it's essential to consult with a healthcare provider or therapist. Nevertheless, for many, these remedies provide a valuable tool for finding emotional balance and harmony in daily life.

- **Methods of Administration and Dosage Guidelines**

- **Incorporating Remedies into Daily Life and Self-Care Practices**

Methods of Administration and Dosage Guidelines for Bach Flower Remedies: Incorporating Remedies into Daily Life and Self-Care Practices

Bach Flower Remedies, a system of natural healing developed by Dr. Edward Bach, offer a gentle and holistic approach to emotional well-being. These remedies are derived from the essence of flowers and plants and are designed to address emotional imbalances and promote overall health. Incorporating Bach Flower Remedies into your daily life and self-care practices can be a transformative journey toward emotional balance and personal growth. In this comprehensive guide, we will explore the various methods of administering Bach Flower Remedies, dosage guidelines, and creative ways to integrate them into your everyday routines.

Understanding the Remedies

Before we delve into the methods of administration and dosage, let's briefly review the essence of Bach Flower Remedies. These remedies consist of 38 different flower essences, each associated with specific emotional states or personality traits. They are prepared by collecting dewdrops from the flowers early in the morning when they are at their most potent. These essences are then diluted and preserved in a solution of water and alcohol to create the final remedies.

The core philosophy of Bach Flower Remedies is based on the

belief that emotional and mental imbalances can have a profound impact on physical health. By addressing emotional issues at their root, these remedies aim to restore emotional equilibrium, thus promoting overall health and well-being.

Methods of Administration

Bach Flower Remedies can be administered in several ways, making them accessible and convenient for individuals of all ages. Here are the primary methods of administration:

1. **Direct Oral Ingestion:** This is the most common and straightforward method. Place two drops of the selected Bach Flower Remedy directly under your tongue, or you can dilute them in a glass of water and sip it throughout the day. It's important to hold the drops under the tongue for a few moments before swallowing to allow for absorption.

2. **Topical Application:** For individuals who may prefer not to ingest the remedies, they can be applied topically. Dilute a few drops of the remedy in a carrier oil (such as almond or coconut oil) and massage it onto the skin. Common application areas include the wrists, temples, and behind the ears.

3. **Incorporation in Food and Drinks:** You can add Bach Flower Remedies to your daily meals or beverages. A few drops in a glass of water, tea, or even your morning smoothie can infuse your meals with the vibrational energy of the remedies.

4. **Environmental Sprays:** Create a room or personal space spray by adding a few drops of Bach Flower Remedy to a spray bottle filled with water. Use this spray to uplift the energy in your environment, such as your home or workspace.

5. **Bathing and Skincare:** Add a few drops of Bach Flower Remedies to your bathwater or skincare products to incorporate them into your self-care routine. This method can be especially soothing for emotional imbalances related to skin conditions or overall well-being.

Dosage Guidelines

Determining the correct dosage of Bach Flower Remedies is essential for achieving optimal results. Here are some general dosage guidelines to consider:

- For acute emotional situations or moments of distress, take two drops of the chosen remedy every 15 minutes, up to four times.

- For ongoing emotional imbalances, take four drops of the remedy four times a day.

- For long-term or chronic emotional issues, continue taking the remedy for several weeks or until the desired emotional balance is achieved.

It's essential to consult a trained Bach Flower practitioner or holistic therapist for personalized recommendations. They can assess your emotional needs and help you select the most appropriate remedies and dosages.

Incorporating Remedies into Daily Life and Self-Care Practices

Now that we've covered the methods of administration and dosage guidelines let's explore creative ways to incorporate Bach Flower Remedies into your daily life and self-care routines:

1. **Morning Ritual:** Start your day with a Bach Flower Remedy by adding a few drops to your morning glass of water or placing them under your tongue. This sets a positive and balanced tone for the day ahead.

2. **Meditation and Mindfulness:** Enhance your meditation or mindfulness practice by taking a Bach Flower Remedy before your session. The remedies can deepen your emotional awareness and inner peace.

3. **Self-Care Pampering:** Treat yourself to a self-care evening with a Bach Flower-infused bath. Add a few drops to your bathwater, light some candles, and relax with soothing music.

4. **Emotional Journaling:** Keep an emotional journal to track your feelings, thoughts, and experiences. Take a Bach Flower Remedy before journaling to encourage self-reflection and insights.

5. **Create Custom Blends:** Mix two or more Bach Flower Remedies to create a personalized blend that addresses your specific emotional needs. Experiment and adjust the blend as your emotional landscape evolves.

6.   **Share with Loved Ones:** Share Bach Flower Remedies with family members or close friends who may benefit from emotional support. A small act of kindness can go a long way in promoting well-being.

7.   **Environmental Enhancement:** Use Bach Flower Remedies to create a positive and harmonious atmosphere in your home. Spritz the remedy-infused room spray in your living space to uplift the energy.

8.   **Travel Companion:** Bach Flower Remedies are convenient for travel. Carry a small bottle in your bag and take them as needed during trips to help you stay emotionally balanced.

9.   **Workplace Support:** Incorporate Bach Flower Remedies into your workplace routine. Keep a remedy spray on your desk or add a few drops to your drinking water to maintain emotional equilibrium during the workday.

10.   **Family and Pet Well-Being:** Bach Flower Remedies are safe for use with children and pets. Consult with a practitioner to select remedies tailored to their emotional needs.

Conclusion: A Holistic Journey to Emotional Balance

Bach Flower Remedies offer a gentle and versatile approach to emotional healing and personal growth. By incorporating these remedies into your daily life and self-care practices, you can create a holistic and transformative journey toward emotional balance.

Remember that Bach Flower Remedies are not a quick fix but a supportive companion on your path to well-being. Be patient with yourself and trust the process of emotional healing. As you infuse your life with the vibrational energy of these remedies, you'll find yourself better equipped to navigate the complexities of emotions and live a more harmonious and fulfilling life.

Chapter : 6

Complementary Approaches and Integration

The disease is, in essence, the result of conflict between soul and mind and will never be eradicated except by spiritual and mental effort.

— Edward Bach

Complementary approaches harmonize physical treatments with spiritual and mental aspects of well-being, acknowledging the soul-mind conflict as vital for holistic health. The integration combines these methods, emphasizing a comprehensive approach that seeks to eradicate disease through spiritual and mental efforts alongside conventional medical treatments.

• Bach Flower Remedies and Other Healing Modalities

In the pursuit of holistic well-being, individuals often explore a variety of healing modalities to address physical, emotional, and spiritual aspects of their health. Among these modalities, Bach Flower Remedies stand out for their focus on emotional balance and healing through the vibrational energy of flowers. However, Bach Flower Remedies can also be seamlessly integrated with other complementary approaches to enhance overall wellness. In this article, we will delve into the world of Bach Flower Remedies and explore how they can be harmoniously combined with other healing modalities to create a more comprehensive approach to well-being.

Understanding Bach Flower Remedies

Before we delve into the integration of Bach Flower Remedies with other healing modalities, let's briefly review what Bach Flower Remedies are and how they work.

Bach Flower Remedies, developed by Dr. Edward Bach in the early 20th century, consist of 38 different flower essences, each associated with a specific emotional state or personality trait. These remedies are prepared by collecting dewdrops from the flowers early in the morning when they are at their most potent. The resulting essences are diluted and preserved in a solution of water and alcohol to create the final remedies.

The core philosophy of Bach Flower Remedies is based on the belief that emotional and mental imbalances can have a profound impact on physical health. These remedies are designed to address these emotional states and help individuals regain emotional equilibrium, thereby promoting overall health.

Exploring Other Healing Modalities

Bach Flower Remedies are just one piece of the holistic wellness puzzle. There is a wide array of complementary and alternative healing modalities available, each with its own unique approach to promoting well-being. Let's take a closer look at some of these modalities and how they can complement the use of Bach Flower Remedies:

1. **Yoga and Mindfulness:** Yoga and mindfulness practices focus on the connection between the mind, body, and spirit. They promote relaxation, reduce

stress, and enhance self-awareness. Combining these practices with Bach Flower Remedies can deepen the emotional healing process.

2. **Meditation:** Meditation is a powerful tool for quieting the mind and cultivating inner peace. When used in conjunction with Bach Flower Remedies, meditation can enhance self-reflection and emotional balance.

3. **Acupuncture:** Acupuncture, a traditional Chinese medicine practice, involves the insertion of thin needles into specific points on the body to restore energy flow. It can complement Bach Flower Remedies by addressing physical and emotional imbalances simultaneously.

4. **Aromatherapy:** Aromatherapy uses essential oils derived from plants to promote relaxation and emotional well-being. Certain essential oils can be used in tandem with Bach Flower Remedies to create a soothing and supportive environment.

5. **Reiki and Energy Healing:** Reiki and other energy healing modalities work with the body's energy fields to promote balance and healing. These practices can align with the vibrational energy of Bach Flower Remedies to enhance emotional and energetic harmony.

6. **Nutritional Therapy:** Proper nutrition is essential for overall health, including emotional well-being. Nutritional therapy can complement Bach Flower Remedies by addressing physical aspects of health that

may be contributing to emotional imbalances.

7. **Traditional Herbal Medicine:** Herbal remedies, like Bach Flower Remedies, draw from the healing power of plants. Combining Bach Flower Remedies with traditional herbal medicine can provide a holistic approach to well-being.

The Synergy of Complementary Approaches

The integration of Bach Flower Remedies with other healing modalities can create a synergy that addresses the whole person—mind, body, and spirit. Here are some key ways in which these approaches can complement each other:

1. **Enhanced Emotional Awareness:** Bach Flower Remedies can help individuals become more attuned to their emotions. When combined with practices like mindfulness and meditation, this awareness can deepen, allowing for greater emotional understanding and healing.

2. **Stress Reduction:** Yoga, meditation, and acupuncture are known for their stress-reducing effects. When used alongside Bach Flower Remedies, they can provide additional support for managing stress and anxiety.

3. **Balanced Energy:** Practices like Reiki and energy healing can balance the body's energy centres, aligning with the vibrational qualities of Bach Flower Remedies to promote emotional and energetic harmony.

4.   **Comprehensive Wellness:** Nutritional therapy and herbal medicine can address physical aspects of health, such as hormonal imbalances or nutritional deficiencies, that may be contributing to emotional issues. This comprehensive approach supports overall wellness.

5.   **Personalized Healing:** The combination of different modalities allows for a personalized approach to healing. A qualified practitioner can assess an individual's unique needs and create a customized wellness plan that includes Bach Flower Remedies and other modalities.

Case Studies in Integration

Let's explore a few case studies to illustrate how individuals have successfully integrated Bach Flower Remedies with other healing modalities:

1.   **Stress and Anxiety Relief:** Jane, a high-stress executive, was experiencing severe anxiety and emotional burnout. She decided to complement her Bach Flower Remedies treatment with regular yoga and meditation sessions. Over time, she noticed a significant reduction in her anxiety levels and a greater sense of emotional balance.

2.   **Chronic Pain and Emotional Healing:** Mark, who suffered from chronic pain due to a medical condition, combined Bach Flower Remedies with acupuncture

treatments. The combination not only helped manage his physical pain but also addressed the emotional distress that often accompanied it.

3. **Hormonal Imbalances:** Neeta, dealing with hormonal imbalances that led to mood swings and irritability, sought the expertise of a holistic practitioner. Together, they created a wellness plan that included Bach Flower Remedies, nutritional therapy, and herbal supplements. Neeta experienced improved emotional stability and overall well-being.

The Role of Practitioners in Integration

For those considering integrating Bach Flower Remedies with other healing modalities, consulting with qualified practitioners is highly recommended. These practitioners can offer expertise in their respective fields and tailor a wellness plan to an individual's unique needs.

A holistic practitioner, such as a naturopathic doctor or integrative wellness coach, can serve as the central point of coordination for an integrated approach to well-being. They can assess an individual's physical and emotional health, recommend appropriate modalities, and monitor progress over time.

Conclusion: Holistic Well-Being through Integration

In the journey toward holistic well-being, there is no one-size-fits-all solution. The integration of Bach Flower Remedies with other healing modalities offers a versatile and personalized approach to addressing physical, emotional, and spiritual aspects of health.

By combining the gentle and vibrational healing of Bach Flower Remedies with practices such as yoga, meditation, acupuncture, and more, individuals can create a comprehensive wellness plan that fosters emotional awareness, reduces stress, balances energy, and supports overall health.

The synergy of these complementary approaches empowers individuals to take an active role in their well-being, fostering a deeper connection with themselves and a greater sense of harmony in their lives. Whether you seek emotional healing, stress reduction, or overall wellness, the integration of Bach Flower Remedies and other healing modalities can be a powerful and transformative journey toward holistic health.

As you embark on your own path to well-being, consider exploring the possibilities of integration and the richness of healing modalities.

- **Using Remedies in Conjunction with Therapy and Counselling**

Using Remedies in Conjunction with Therapy and Counselling: A Holistic Approach to Emotional Well-Being

In the quest for emotional healing and personal growth, individuals often turn to therapy and counselling as a supportive framework to address deep-seated emotional issues and gain insights into their lives. Therapy provides a safe space to explore one's feelings, thoughts, and behaviours, and it can be instrumental in promoting emotional well-being. An emerging trend in this field is the integration of complementary approaches like Bach Flower

Remedies with traditional therapy and counselling. In this article, we will delve into the benefits of combining these modalities and how they can work synergistically to support holistic emotional healing.

The Power of Therapy and Counselling

Therapy and counselling, whether it's cognitive-behavioural therapy, talk therapy, psychoanalysis, or any other approach, are valuable tools for individuals facing emotional challenges. These modalities offer several benefits:

1. **Professional Guidance:** Therapists and counsellors are trained to provide evidence-based guidance and support for various emotional and psychological issues.

2. **Safe and Confidential Space:** Therapy sessions create a safe and confidential environment where individuals can express their deepest thoughts and emotions without judgment.

3. **Self-Exploration:** Therapy encourages self-reflection and exploration, helping individuals gain insight into their emotional patterns and behaviours.

4. **Tools and Coping Strategies:** Therapists often teach practical coping strategies and tools to manage and overcome emotional difficulties.

5. **Long-Term Well-Being:** Therapy can promote long-term emotional well-being by addressing the root causes of emotional distress.

The Role of Bach Flower Remedies

Bach Flower Remedies, developed by Dr. Edward Bach, consist of 38 flower essences, each associated with specific emotional states or personality traits. These remedies are designed to restore emotional equilibrium and promote healing. When integrated with therapy and counselling, Bach Flower Remedies can provide additional support for emotional healing in several ways:

1. **Enhancing Emotional Awareness:** Bach Flower Remedies can help individuals become more aware of their emotional states and patterns. This heightened awareness can be valuable during therapy sessions, allowing individuals to delve deeper into their emotions.

2. **Facilitating Emotional Release:** Certain Bach Flower Remedies, such as "Holly" for anger or "Cherry Plum" for fear of losing control, can assist individuals in safely exploring and releasing intense emotions during therapy.

3. **Emotional Resilience:** Bach Flower Remedies can bolster emotional resilience, helping individuals better cope with the challenges and emotional revelations that often arise in therapy.

4. **Supporting Emotional Processing:** Therapy can stir up deep emotions and memories. Bach Flower Remedies can support the emotional processing and integration of these experiences.

Integration in Practice

Here's a practical overview of how Bach Flower Remedies can be integrated with therapy and counselling:

1. **Consultation with a Practitioner:** Start by consulting with a trained Bach Flower practitioner or holistic therapist. They can assess your emotional needs and recommend specific remedies that align with your therapeutic goals.

2. **Incorporate Remedies into Daily Routine:** Take the prescribed Bach Flower Remedies as part of your daily routine, following the practitioner's instructions. These remedies are typically taken as drops under the tongue or diluted in water.

3. **Inform Your Therapist or Counsellor:** It's essential to communicate with your therapist or counsellor about your use of Bach Flower Remedies. They can tailor their approach to complement the remedies and help you maximize the benefits of both modalities.

4. **Use Remedies During Sessions:** Some individuals find it helpful to take a dose of Bach Flower Remedies shortly before or during therapy sessions to enhance their emotional receptivity and processing.

5. **Self-Reflection and Journaling:** Incorporate self-reflection and journaling into your routine to track your emotional progress. This can provide valuable insights during therapy sessions.

6. **Regular Feedback and Adjustments:** Stay in touch with both your Bach Flower practitioner and therapist to provide feedback on your emotional experiences. Adjustments to the remedies or therapy approach can be made as needed.

Benefits of Integration

The integration of Bach Flower Remedies with therapy and counselling can yield several benefits:

1. **Enhanced Emotional Healing:** Combining these modalities allows for a more holistic approach to emotional healing, addressing both the conscious and subconscious aspects of emotional distress.

2. **Faster Progress:** Bach Flower Remedies can accelerate emotional healing, potentially reducing the duration of therapy.

3. **Deeper Insights:** The heightened emotional awareness facilitated by the remedies can lead to deeper insights and breakthroughs during therapy sessions.

4. **Emotional Resilience:** Individuals often find they have increased emotional resilience and coping skills when using Bach Flower Remedies alongside therapy.

5. **Personalized Care:** The integration approach is highly personalized, allowing individuals to tailor their healing journey to their unique needs.

Conclusion: A Holistic Path to Emotional Well-Being

In the quest for emotional healing and personal growth, it's important to recognize that no single approach is universally effective. The integration of Bach Flower Remedies with therapy and counselling provides a holistic path to emotional well-being, addressing emotional imbalances on multiple levels.

Whether you're working through trauma, managing anxiety or depression, or simply seeking greater self-awareness, the synergy of these modalities can empower you to navigate your emotional landscape more effectively. The gentle yet transformative nature of Bach Flower Remedies, when combined with the professional guidance of therapy and counselling, offers a comprehensive approach to emotional healing and personal growth.

As you embark on your journey of emotional well-being, consider the possibilities of integrating Bach Flower Remedies with therapy or counselling. Embrace the power of self-discovery and emotional transformation as you work towards a more balanced and fulfilling life.

- **Custom Blends and Combination Remedies for Complex Emotional Needs**

Custom Blends and Combination Remedies for Complex Emotional Needs

In the pursuit of emotional well-being and balance, individuals often face complex emotional states and challenges. While Bach Flower Remedies provide a powerful tool for addressing specific emotional issues, the art of creating custom blends and using combination remedies offers a versatile approach to addressing complex emotional needs. In this guide, we will explore how to craft custom blends and leverage combination remedies to support profound emotional healing and personal growth.

Understanding the Essence of Bach Flower Remedies

Bach Flower Remedies, developed by Dr. Edward Bach, consist of 38 different flower essences, each associated with a specific emotional state or personality trait. These remedies are designed to address emotional imbalances and promote overall health. To effectively create custom blends and utilize combination remedies, it's essential to have a fundamental understanding of the core remedies and their corresponding emotional states.

The Power of Custom Blends

Custom blends are personalized combinations of Bach Flower Remedies tailored to an individual's unique emotional landscape. The process involves selecting specific remedies that resonate with the individual's emotional challenges and aspirations. Custom blends offer several advantages for addressing complex emotional needs:

1. **Personalization:** Custom blends are uniquely tailored to address the precise emotional issues a person is experiencing. This personalization ensures that the remedies resonate with the individual on a deep level.

2. **Comprehensive Support:** Complex emotional needs often involve multiple emotional states. Custom

blends can encompass a range of remedies to provide comprehensive support.

3. **Flexibility:** As emotions evolve and change over time, custom blends can be adjusted and modified to adapt to shifting emotional needs.

4. **Empowerment:** Creating a custom blend empowers individuals to take an active role in their emotional healing and personal growth. It fosters a sense of agency and self-awareness.

The Process of Creating Custom Blends

Crafting custom blends of Bach Flower Remedies is an art that requires a thoughtful and intuitive approach. Here are the key steps to create a custom blend:

1. **Self-Reflection:** Begin by engaging in self-reflection to identify the complex emotional issues you are facing. Consider the specific emotions, thoughts, and behaviours that you want to address.

2. **Consult with a Practitioner:** While creating a custom blend is a personal journey, it's advisable to consult with a trained Bach Flower practitioner or holistic therapist. They can offer guidance and insights based on their expertise.

3. **Selecting Remedies:** Based on your self-reflection and consultation, choose the individual Bach Flower Remedies that resonate with your emotional challenges. Each remedy corresponds to a specific emotional state.

4. **Dosage and Mixing:** Determine the appropriate dosage for each remedy and combine them in a mixing bottle. Typically, each remedy is used in a 30ml mixing bottle with a few drops of each selected remedy.

5. **Water and Preservative:** Fill the mixing bottle with spring water or mineral water, leaving some space at the top. Add a small amount of preservative, such as brandy or apple cider vinegar, to keep the blend fresh.

6. **Personal Affirmation:** Some individuals like to add a personal affirmation or intention to their custom blend. This affirmation can be written on a piece of paper and placed near the mixing bottle.

7. **Taking the Blend:** Take four drops of your custom blend under the tongue, at least four times a day. It's important to follow a consistent routine to experience the full benefits.

8. **Self-Monitoring:** Keep a journal to track your emotional progress while using the custom blend. Document any shifts in emotions, thoughts, and behaviours.

The Power of Combination Remedies

In addition to custom blends, Bach Flower Remedies also offer pre-made combination remedies designed to address specific emotional themes or situations. Combination remedies are carefully crafted blends of multiple Bach Flower Remedies that work synergistically to provide comprehensive emotional support.

Combination remedies are particularly useful for individuals dealing with complex emotional needs, as they target a range of emotional states simultaneously. Some common themes for combination remedies include stress relief, confidence-building, and emotional balance.

Choosing the Right Combination Remedy

When selecting a combination remedy for complex emotional needs, consider the following factors:

1. **Identify the Core Issue:** Determine the primary emotional issue or theme you want to address. Combination remedies are typically labelled to indicate their purpose, making it easier to select the right one.

2. **Read the Descriptions:** Read the descriptions and indications provided on the combination remedy packaging. These descriptions will help you align the remedy with your specific emotional challenges.

3. **Consult with a Practitioner:** If you're unsure which combination remedy is suitable, consult with a Bach Flower practitioner or holistic therapist. They can offer personalized recommendations based on your needs.

Incorporating Custom Blends and Combination Remedies

Here are some practical ways to incorporate custom blends and combination remedies into your daily life:

1. **Morning Ritual:** Start your day by taking your custom blend or combination remedy. This sets a positive emotional tone for the day ahead.

2.   **Meditation and Reflection:** Use your remedies as part of your meditation or self-reflection practice. The vibrational energy of the remedies can enhance your emotional awareness.

3.   **Workplace Support:** Keep your remedies on your desk or in your workspace. They can help you maintain emotional equilibrium during the workday.

4.   **Evening Routine:** Take your remedies as part of your evening self-care routine. This can assist in emotional processing and relaxation before bedtime.

5.   **Travel Companion:** Carry a small bottle of your custom blend or combination remedy with you when travelling. It can provide emotional support during unfamiliar situations.

6.   **Family and Relationships:** Share remedies with family members or loved ones who may benefit from emotional support. They can be used to create a harmonious emotional environment.

Conclusion: A Holistic Approach to Complex Emotional Needs

Addressing complex emotional needs is a journey of self-discovery and healing. Custom blends and combination remedies offer versatile and personalized approaches to emotional well-being. Whether you choose to create a custom blend tailored to your unique emotional landscape or opt for a combination remedy designed for specific themes, the power of Bach Flower Remedies lies in their ability to support profound emotional healing and personal growth.

As you incorporate custom blends and combination remedies into your daily life, remember that emotional healing is a gradual process. Trust in the wisdom of these remedies to guide you toward a more balanced and fulfilling emotional state. Embrace the journey of self-awareness and transformation.

Chapter : 7

Advanced Applications and Techniques

Five hundred years before Christ, some physicians of ancient India, working under the influence of the Lord Buddha, advanced the art of healing to so perfect a state that they were able to abolish surgery, although the surgery of their time was as efficient, or more so, than that of the present day.
- Edward Bach

Edward Bach developed Bach Flower Remedies, a form of alternative medicine. While there's no direct correlation between these remedies and advanced medical applications or surgical techniques, Bach believed in addressing underlying personality traits and emotional imbalances as a means of promoting overall health and well-being, which is a holistic approach to healing.

- Type Remedies: Addressing Underlying Personality Traits

Advanced Applications and Techniques for Bach Flower Remedies: Type Remedies - Addressing Underlying Personality Traits

Bach Flower Remedies, developed by Dr. Edward Bach, offer a profound approach to emotional healing and personal growth. While these remedies are commonly used to address specific emotional states, advanced practitioners and enthusiasts often delve deeper into the system by exploring "Type Remedies." Type Remedies go beyond individual emotional states and are tailored to address underlying personality traits. In this comprehensive guide, we will explore advanced applications and techniques for Bach Flower Remedies, with a special focus on Type Remedies and their potential to foster holistic transformation.

Bach Flower Remedies: A Brief Overview

Before we dive into advanced applications, let's briefly revisit the essence of Bach Flower Remedies. This system of natural healing comprises 38 different flower essences, each associated with specific emotional states or personality traits. These remedies are designed to address emotional imbalances and promote overall well-being by restoring emotional equilibrium.

Dr. Bach's philosophy rested on the belief that addressing the root causes of emotional distress is essential for achieving lasting physical and emotional health. Bach Flower Remedies are renowned for their gentle yet profound effects on the human psyche.

Advanced Applications of Bach Flower Remedies

Advanced applications of Bach Flower Remedies extend beyond addressing surface-level emotional concerns. They involve a deeper exploration of one's personality traits, tendencies, and underlying emotional patterns. Here are some advanced techniques and applications:

1. Type Remedies: Addressing Underlying Personality Traits

Type Remedies, also known as Constitutional Remedies or Personality Remedies, form the cornerstone of advanced Bach Flower Therapy. These remedies are crafted to address an individual's inherent personality traits and characteristics, which may contribute to emotional imbalances and life challenges. Type Remedies are particularly valuable for individuals seeking profound personal growth and self-awareness.

Understanding Type Remedies

Type Remedies are not based solely on the immediate emotional state but on the individual's long-standing, recurring patterns of behaviour and thought. These patterns often underlie chronic emotional issues and can impact various aspects of one's life, including relationships, career, and personal development.

For example, an individual with a Type Remedy related to perfectionism may constantly strive for perfection in their work and life, leading to chronic stress and anxiety. By addressing the underlying perfectionist tendencies, the individual can experience lasting emotional balance and personal growth.

Identifying Your Type Remedy

Identifying your Type Remedy requires a deep and honest self-assessment. Here are some steps to help you recognize your underlying personality traits:

1. **Self-Reflection:** Engage in self-reflection to identify recurring patterns of behaviour, thought, and emotion in your life. Pay attention to situations that trigger certain reactions.

2. **Consult with a Practitioner:** Consider consulting with a trained Bach Flower practitioner or holistic therapist who specializes in Type Remedies. They can provide insights based on their expertise.

3. **Questioning Beliefs:** Examine your core beliefs and values. Ask yourself why you respond to situations or challenges in specific ways. Are there deep-seated beliefs driving your behaviour?

4. **Patterns in Different Areas:** Observe if similar personality traits or patterns emerge in different areas of your life, such as relationships, work, and personal development.

Common Type Remedies and Their Characteristics

While there are numerous types of Remedies, here are a few common ones and their associated characteristics:

1. **Perfectionist (Agrimony):** Perfectionists tend to set high standards for themselves and others. They may struggle with inner turmoil and hide their true emotions behind a cheerful facade.

2. **Overachiever (Vervain):** Overachievers are driven and passionate about their causes. However, their enthusiasm can lead to burnout and a tendency to overextend themselves.

3. **People-Pleaser (Centaury):** People-pleasers have difficulty saying no and often prioritize others' needs over their own. They may struggle with feelings of being taken advantage of.

4. **Loner (Water Violet):** Loners' value their independence and self-sufficiency. While they may appear self-assured, they can sometimes come across as aloof or

distant.

5.   **Self-Doubter (Larch):** Self-doubters lack confidence in their abilities and may fear failure. They often hesitate to take on challenges or opportunities.

Creating a Type Remedy Blend

Once you've identified your Type Remedy, you can create a custom blend using the corresponding Bach Flower Remedies. Here's a general process to create a Type Remedy blend:

1.   **Select the Remedies:** Choose the Bach Flower Remedies that correspond to your identified Type Remedy. This typically involves two to four remedies.

2.   **Dosage and Mixing:** Determine the appropriate dosage for each remedy and mix them in a 30ml mixing bottle. A typical dosage might be two drops of each selected remedy.

3.   **Water and Preservative:** Fill the mixing bottle with spring water or mineral water, leaving some space at the top. Add a small amount of preservative, such as brandy or apple cider vinegar.

4.   **Personal Affirmation:** Consider adding a personal affirmation or intention to your Type Remedy blend. This affirmation can be written on a piece of paper and placed near the mixing bottle.

5.   **Taking the Blend:** Take four drops of your Type Remedy blend under the tongue at least four times a

day. Consistency is key to experiencing the full benefits.

Type Remedies in Practice

Let's explore a practical example to illustrate the use of Type Remedies in addressing underlying personality traits:

Case Study: The Perfectionist

Neeta, a high-achieving professional, identified herself as a perfectionist through self-reflection and consultation with a Bach Flower practitioner. Her perfectionism led to chronic stress and anxiety, affecting her work and personal life.

After identifying her Type Remedy as Agrimony, Neeta created a custom blend that included Agrimony along with other remedies to address specific emotional nuances. She took the blend regularly as directed.

Over time, Neeta noticed significant changes in her behaviour and emotional well-being. She became more aware of her tendency to hide her true feelings behind a cheerful facade, and she started to express her emotions more authentically. Her chronic stress decreased, and she found greater emotional balance.

Conclusion: A Holistic Path to Personal Growth

Type Remedies are a powerful tool within the Bach Flower Remedies system, offering a path to deeper self-awareness and personal growth. By addressing underlying personality traits and patterns, individuals can experience profound shifts in their emotional well-being and life experiences.

Remember that identifying and working with Type Remedies is

a journey of self-discovery. It requires patience, self-compassion, and a commitment to personal growth. Whether you're a seasoned practitioner or new to Bach Flower Remedies, the exploration of Type Remedies offers an opportunity to delve deeper into the transformative power of these natural essences.

As you embark on this holistic path to personal growth, embrace the process of self-exploration and self-acceptance. Type Remedies are a valuable resource on your journey toward emotional balance and a more authentic and fulfilling life.

- **Exploring the Seven Emotional Groups**

Bach Flower Remedies, created by Dr. Edward Bach, have been widely recognized for their remarkable ability to address emotional imbalances and promote holistic well-being. Beyond their individual applications, practitioners and enthusiasts have delved into advanced techniques, such as exploring the Seven Emotional Groups. This approach offers a deeper understanding of emotional patterns and provides a more comprehensive tool for emotional healing and personal growth. In this comprehensive guide, we will explore advanced applications and techniques by delving into the Seven Emotional Groups in Bach Flower Remedies.

Understanding the Seven Emotional Groups

Dr. Edward Bach, in his exploration of emotions and their relationship to health, categorized the 38 Bach Flower Remedies into Seven Emotional Groups. Each group represents a broad emotional theme or pattern, allowing for a more nuanced and holistic approach to emotional healing. Here are the Seven Emotional Groups:

1. **Fear Group:** This group addresses various fear-related emotions, such as fear of the unknown, fear of illness, or fear of losing control. Remedies in this group include Mimulus, Aspen, Rock Rose, Cherry Plum, and Red Chestnut.

2. **Uncertainty Group**: Emotions related to uncertainty and indecision are the focus here. This group includes remedies like Cerato, Scleranthus, Gentian, Gorse, and Hornbeam.

3. **Insufficient Interest in Present Circumstances Group:** Individuals in this group may be emotionally disconnected or disinterested in their current life circumstances. Remedies include Clematis, Honeysuckle, Wild Rose, Olive, and White Chestnut.

4. **Loneliness Group:** Loneliness, isolation, and feelings of being unloved are addressed in this group. Remedies like Water Violet, Impatiens, Heather, and Chicory are included.

5. **Over-Sensitivity to Influences and Ideas Group:** This group encompasses individuals who are highly sensitive to external influences and are easily influenced by others' opinions or emotions. Remedies include Agrimony, Centaury, Walnut, Holly, and Larch.

6. **Despondency or Despair Group**: Emotions related to

deep sadness, hopelessness, and despair are the focus here. Remedies include Pine, Elm, Sweet Chestnut, Star of Bethlehem, and Willow.

7. **Over-Care for Welfare of Others Group:** Individuals in this group tend to overextend themselves in caring for others but may neglect their own well-being. Remedies like Red Chestnut, Chicory, Vervain, Vine, and Beech are included.

Advanced Techniques Using the Seven Emotional Groups

Exploring the Seven Emotional Groups opens up advanced techniques for practitioners and individuals seeking deeper emotional healing and personal growth. Here's how you can utilize this approach:

1. Identifying Dominant Emotional Groups:

Begin by identifying which of the Seven Emotional Groups resonates most with your emotional landscape or the emotional patterns of the person you are assisting. This identification can provide valuable insights into the root causes of emotional imbalances.

For example, if you consistently find yourself experiencing fear-related emotions, you may belong to the Fear Group. Recognizing this can guide you toward remedies such as Mimulus or Aspen, which specifically address these fears.

2. Creating Comprehensive Blends:

Rather than addressing individual emotional states one at a time, consider creating comprehensive blends that include remedies from the dominant Emotional Group. These blends provide holistic support for your emotional well-being.

Suppose you belong to the Loneliness Group and frequently experience feelings of isolation and unloved. In that case, you might create a blend that combines remedies like Water Violet, Impatiens, and Heather to address the various facets of loneliness.

3. Tailoring Remedies to Subtle Nuances:

Within each Emotional Group, there can be subtle nuances in emotional patterns. Advanced practitioners often delve into these nuances to fine-tune remedy selection.

For example, if you are addressing over-sensitivity within the Over-Sensitivity to Influences and Ideas Group, you might choose remedies like Holly for intense anger and Walnut for adaptability to external influences. Tailoring remedies to these nuances enhances their effectiveness.

4. Supporting Personal Growth:

The Seven Emotional Groups offer a roadmap for personal growth. By identifying your dominant group and working with corresponding remedies, you can address deep-seated emotional patterns that may be hindering your personal development.

For instance, if you belong to the Over-Care for Welfare of Others Group, you can use remedies like Vervain to balance your desire to help others while maintaining healthy boundaries.

Practical Application: A Case Study

Let's explore a case study to illustrate the practical application of the Seven Emotional Groups:

Case Study: Neeta's Over-Sensitivity

Neeta identifies herself as belonging to the Over-Sensitivity to Influences and Ideas Group. She often finds herself overwhelmed by external stimuli, is easily influenced by others' opinions, and experiences intense anger in response to perceived injustices.

Advanced Technique: Comprehensive Blend

Neeta creates a comprehensive blend that includes remedies from the Over-Sensitivity to Influences and Ideas Group:

- Agrimony: To address her tendency to hide her true emotions behind a cheerful facade.

- Centaury: To help her assert healthy boundaries and say no when necessary.

- Walnut: To enhance her adaptability to external influences.

- Holly: To work on her intense anger and resentment.

- Larch: To boost her self-confidence and reduce feelings of inadequacy.

Neeta takes this blend regularly and notices significant improvements in her emotional well-being. She becomes more self-aware, better able to manage her sensitivity, and experiences enhanced emotional balance.

Conclusion: A Holistic Approach to Emotional Healing

Exploring the Seven Emotional Groups in Bach Flower Remedies offers an advanced and holistic approach to emotional healing and personal growth. By identifying dominant emotional patterns and selecting remedies from the corresponding group, individuals can address deep-seated emotional imbalances that may have been challenging to resolve with individual remedies alone.

As you embark on your journey of advanced Bach Flower Remedies, remember that self-awareness and patience are key. The Seven Emotional Groups provide a rich tapestry for understanding and transforming your emotional landscape. Embrace this holistic approach to emotional healing and personal growth, and trust in the transformative power of Bach Flower Remedies to support your journey toward emotional balance and a more fulfilling life.

- **Recent Research and Scientific Advancements in Bach Flower Remedies**

    1. **Consult Experts:** Reach out to experts in the field of Bach Flower Remedies or alternative medicine. They may be aware of recent developments and can provide insights or direct you to credible sources.

    2. **Check Bach Flower Remedies Websites:** Visit websites and resources related to Bach Flower Remedies, including those of authorized practitioners, Bach Centre, and Bach flower remedy manufacturers.

These sources often provide updates on research and developments within the field.

3. **Read Books and Publications:** Look for books, magazines, or publications dedicated to Bach Flower Remedies. Authors and practitioners may share recent research findings or advancements in their work.

4. **Join Bach Flower Remedies Communities:** Join online forums, social media groups, or communities dedicated to Bach Flower Remedies. These platforms often discuss recent research findings and experiences with the remedies.

5. **Consult a Bach Flower Practitioner:** Bach Flower Practitioners may have insights into recent research or developments in the field. They can provide guidance based on their knowledge and experience.

6. **Stay Updated:** Subscribe to newsletters or mailing lists of organizations or individuals involved in Bach Flower Remedies. They may send out updates on research findings and advancements.

When exploring recent research, it's important to critically evaluate the sources and consider the methodology, sample size, and relevance of the studies. This will help you make informed decisions about incorporating Bach Flower Remedies into your wellness practices or understanding their potential benefits.

Chapter : 8

Nurturing Emotional Well-being

Health depends on being in harmony with our souls
- Edward Bach

Emotional well-being this statement underscores the importance of aligning our inner selves, our emotional states, and our souls. It suggests that true health and well-being extend beyond just physical health; they encompass the alignment of our emotional and spiritual aspects.

Nurturing emotional well-being often involves exploring our inner selves, understanding our emotions, and striving for inner harmony. When we are in harmony with our souls, we are more likely to experience emotional balance, peace of mind, and a sense of purpose—all essential components of overall well-being.

Dr. Bach's work with Bach Flower Remedies aligns with this philosophy by offering a holistic approach to emotional healing and well-being, aiming to help individuals find that harmony within themselves.

- **Embracing Emotional Wellness: Mind, Body, and Spirit**

Embracing Emotional Wellness: A Holistic Approach to Mind, Body, and Spirit

Emotional wellness is an integral part of our overall well-being, encompassing our mental, emotional, physical, and spiritual health. It's about finding balance and harmony within ourselves, even in the face of life's challenges. In this guide, we'll explore the concept of emotional wellness and how it can be nurtured through a holistic approach that integrates the mind, body, and spirit.

Understanding Emotional Wellness

Emotional wellness goes beyond just the absence of mental health issues; it encompasses a positive state of emotional health and resilience. It involves:

1. **Self-Awareness:** Understanding our emotions, their triggers, and their impact on our thoughts and actions.

2. **Emotional Regulation:** The ability to manage and express emotions in a healthy way without suppressing or overwhelming ourselves.

3. **Stress Management:** Effectively coping with stressors and challenges in our daily lives.

4. **Healthy Relationships:** Building and maintaining fulfilling connections with others, marked by empathy, communication, and support.

5. **Life Satisfaction:** Experiencing a sense of purpose, fulfilment, and contentment in our lives.

The Mind: Nurturing Emotional Wellness

1. **Mindfulness and Meditation:** Practicing mindfulness and meditation can help us become more aware of our thoughts and emotions, reducing stress and promoting emotional regulation.

2.   **Cognitive Behavioural Therapy (CBT):** CBT techniques can help reduce negative thought patterns and improve emotional well-being.

3.   **Emotional Intelligence (EQ):** Developing emotional intelligence skills can enhance our self-awareness, empathy, and relationship-building abilities.

4.   **Journaling:** Keeping an emotional journal can help us process and understand our feelings and experiences.

The Body: Physical Health and Emotional Wellness

1.   **Nutrition:** A balanced diet rich in nutrients can support our emotional health. Foods like fatty fish, leafy greens, and berries have been linked to improved mood.

2.   **Exercise:** Regular physical activity releases endorphins, the body's natural mood elevators, promoting a sense of well-being.

3.   **Sleep:** Quality sleep is essential for emotional regulation and mental clarity. Establishing a sleep routine can improve emotional wellness.

4.   **Mind-Body Practices:** Techniques like yoga, tai chi, and Qi Gong combine physical movement with mindfulness, promoting emotional balance.

The Spirit: Nurturing the Soul

1.   **Spiritual Practices:** Engaging in spiritual practices that resonate with you, whether it's prayer, meditation, or spending time in nature, can nurture the spirit.

2. **Creative Expression:** Pursuing creative hobbies like art, music, or writing can be a source of emotional release and fulfilment.

3. **Gratitude:** Cultivating a sense of gratitude for the present moment and the blessings in our lives can foster emotional well-being.

Holistic Approaches to Emotional Wellness

1. **Bach Flower Remedies:** Bach Flower Remedies, derived from flower essences, can address emotional imbalances and promote emotional wellness. These remedies, like Rescue Remedy for stress or Aspen for anxiety, can be incorporated into your daily routine.

2. **Aromatherapy:** The use of essential oils in aromatherapy can have a calming or uplifting effect on emotions. Lavender, for instance, is known for its calming properties.

3. **Holistic Therapies:** Practices like acupuncture, massage therapy, and energy healing can help release emotional blockages and restore balance.

4. **Social Support:** Building strong social connections and seeking support from friends, family, or support groups can be essential for emotional wellness.

Embracing Emotional Wellness: A Journey

Embracing emotional wellness is an ongoing journey. It's important to remember that emotional well-being is not about eliminating negative emotions but rather learning to navigate them in a healthy way. Here are some final thoughts and encouragement for your emotional wellness journey:

1. **Self-Compassion:** Be kind and compassionate toward yourself. Emotions, both positive and negative, are a natural part of being human.

2. **Seek Professional Help:** If you're struggling with your emotional wellness, consider seeking support from a therapist or counsellor who can provide guidance and tools to navigate your emotions.

3. **Practice Patience:** Emotional growth takes time. Be patient with yourself as you work on developing emotional awareness and resilience.

4. **Embrace Balance**: Balance is key to emotional wellness. Strive for balance in your daily life, making time for self-care, work, relationships, and leisure.

5. **Celebrate Progress:** Celebrate your successes, no matter how small they may seem. Each step forward in your emotional wellness journey is a significant achievement.

Remember that emotional wellness is a dynamic and evolving process. By integrating mind, body, and spirit and incorporating holistic approaches into your life, you can nurture your emotional well-being and experience a greater sense of balance, resilience, and fulfilment.

- ## Creating Rituals and Practices for Emotional Balance

Emotional balance is a precious state of well-being that allows us to navigate life's ups and downs with resilience and grace. One powerful way to cultivate and maintain emotional balance is by incorporating rituals and practices into our daily lives. In this guide, we will explore the art of creating rituals and practices that nurture your inner harmony, fostering emotional equilibrium and well-being.

The Power of Rituals and Practices

Rituals and practices are intentional and purposeful activities that help us connect with ourselves, the world around us, and the deeper aspects of our being. When it comes to emotional balance, these rituals serve several vital purposes:

1. **Grounding and Centring:** Rituals provide a sense of stability and grounding, helping us stay rooted in the present moment.

2. **Emotional Release:** Certain practices, such as journaling or creative expression, offer a healthy outlet for processing and releasing pent-up emotions.

3. **Self-Care:** Engaging in rituals and practices is an act of self-care, demonstrating our commitment to our emotional well-being.

4. **Mindfulness and Awareness:** Many rituals promote mindfulness and self-awareness, allowing us to observe our emotions without judgment.

5. **Stress Reduction:** Regular rituals and practices can reduce stress and anxiety, promoting emotional equilibrium.

Creating Your Emotional Balance Toolkit

To craft rituals and practices that nurture emotional balance, it's essential to build a toolkit of activities that resonate with you. Here are some key elements to consider:

1. **Self-Reflection:** Begin by reflecting on your emotional needs and challenges. What emotions do you frequently grapple with? What activities or practices have helped you in the past?

2. **Personal Interests:** Incorporate activities that align with your personal interests and passions. Doing what you love enhances the effectiveness of your rituals.

3. **Variety:** Include a variety of practices in your toolkit to address different emotional states. For example, meditation can help with stress, while creative expression can aid in processing complex emotions.

4. **Consistency:** Commit to practising your chosen rituals regularly. Consistency is key to experiencing the full benefits of these activities.

Creating Your Emotional Balance Rituals and Practices

Now, let's delve into specific rituals and practices you can incorporate into your daily life to nurture emotional balance:

1. Mindfulness Meditation:

Mindfulness meditation involves paying focused, non-judgmental attention to the present moment. It is highly effective in reducing stress and promoting emotional awareness. Create a daily meditation ritual, even if it's just for a few minutes, to centre yourself and observe your emotions without attachment.

2. Gratitude Journaling:

Each day, write down three things you're grateful for. This simple practice shifts your focus from what's lacking to what's abundant in your life, fostering a positive outlook and emotional balance.

3. Creative Expression:

Engage in a creative outlet that speaks to you, whether it's painting, writing, dancing, or playing a musical instrument. Creative expression allows you to channel your emotions and thoughts into a tangible form.

4. Breathwork:

Practice deep breathing exercises to calm your nervous system and reduce stress. The 4-7-8 technique, where you inhale for four seconds, hold for seven seconds, and exhale for eight seconds, is particularly effective.

5. Yoga and Tai Chi:

Yoga and Tai Chi combine physical movement with mindfulness, promoting relaxation and emotional balance. Consider attending classes or incorporating these practices into your daily routine.

6. Nature Connection:

Spend time in nature regularly. Nature has a calming and rejuvenating effect on our emotions. Go for walks, hike, or simply sit in a park and soak in the natural surroundings.

7. Emotional Release Ritual:

Design a ritual to release pent-up emotions. This could involve writing a letter to yourself or someone else (without the intention of sending it), practising a cathartic scream, or engaging in a releasing meditation.

8. Affirmations:

Create positive affirmations that resonate with you and repeat them daily. Affirmations can help rewire your thought patterns and foster emotional well-being.

9. Digital Detox:

Set aside dedicated times during the day to disconnect from digital devices. The constant influx of information and notifications can contribute to emotional overwhelm.

10. Visualization:

Practice guided visualizations to create a mental sanctuary where you can retreat to find peace and emotional balance whenever needed.

11. Acts of Kindness:

Perform acts of kindness for others regularly. Acts of kindness boost your own sense of well-being and can improve your emotional state.

12. Ritual of Release and Renewal:

Design a monthly or seasonal ritual where you symbolically release old emotional baggage and invite fresh, positive energy into your life.

13. Bach Flower Remedies:

Incorporate Bach Flower Remedies into your daily routine. These natural remedies can address specific emotional imbalances and promote emotional equilibrium. For example, Rescue Remedy is a well-known remedy for stress and anxiety.

14. Mindful Eating:

Practice mindful eating by savouring each bite, eating without distractions, and paying attention to your body's hunger and fullness cues. Your emotional state is closely tied to your relationship with food.

15. Self-Compassion:

Make self-compassion a daily practice. Treat yourself with the same kindness and understanding that you would offer to a dear friend.

Building Your Rituals into Daily Life

To make these rituals and practices a consistent part of your life, consider the following tips:

1. **Create a Routine:** Set aside specific times each day or week for your chosen rituals. Having a routine makes it easier to stick with your practices.

2. **Start Small:** Begin with manageable increments of time. Even dedicating five minutes to a practice each day can yield benefits.

3. **Accountability:** Share your commitment with a friend or loved one who can hold you accountable and offer support.

4. **Visual Reminders:** Use visual cues or reminders, such as post-it notes or phone alarms, to prompt you to engage in your chosen practices.

5. **Be Patient:** Emotional balance is a journey. Be patient with yourself as you integrate these rituals into your life. Progress may be gradual.

Conclusion: Nurturing Emotional Harmony

Emotional balance is not a destination but a continuous journey. By creating rituals and practices that resonate with your unique needs and preferences, you can nurture your inner harmony and build emotional resilience. These practices serve as tools to help you navigate life's emotional terrain with grace and equanimity.

Remember that there is no one-size-fits-all approach to emotional balance. Your journey is personal, and your rituals and practices should reflect what brings you peace and fulfilment. Embrace the process, celebrate your progress, and hold space for the ongoing cultivation of emotional well-being in your life.

- **Long-Term Use and Maintenance of Emotional Health**

Emotional health is not a destination; it's a lifelong journey. Just as we maintain physical health through diet, exercise, and regular check-ups, we must also nurture our emotional well-being consistently. In this comprehensive guide, we'll explore the importance of long-term emotional health and provide practical strategies for its maintenance.

The Significance of Long-Term Emotional Health

Emotional health plays a fundamental role in our overall well-being. It influences our thoughts, actions, and relationships. Long-term emotional health encompasses not only the absence of mental illness but also the cultivation of positive emotions, resilience, and the ability to cope with life's challenges. Here's why it's crucial:

1. **Resilience:** Emotional well-being equips us with the resilience to bounce back from adversity, stress, and setbacks.

2. **Quality of Life:** A stable emotional state enhances our quality of life, leading to greater happiness, satisfaction, and fulfilment.

3. **Healthy Relationships:** Emotional health fosters healthy relationships, as it enables effective communication, empathy, and conflict resolution.

4. **Physical Health:** Our emotional state affects our physical health. Chronic stress, for example, can lead to various health issues.

5. **Life Satisfaction:** Long-term emotional well-being contributes to an overall sense of life satisfaction and well-rounded wellness.

Strategies for Long-Term Emotional Health

To sustain and nurture emotional health over the long term, consider incorporating the following strategies into your daily life:

1. Self-Care Routine:

1. **Regular Exercise:** Engage in physical activity that you enjoy, whether it's jogging, yoga, dancing, or hiking. Exercise releases endorphins, which are natural mood lifters.

2. **Balanced Diet:** Eat a balanced diet rich in whole foods, including fruits, vegetables, lean proteins, and whole grains. Proper nutrition supports both physical and emotional health.

3. **Adequate Sleep:** Prioritize sleep by establishing a consistent sleep schedule and creating a relaxing bedtime routine.

4. **Mindful Eating:** Practice mindful eating by savouring each bite and paying attention to your body's hunger and fullness cues.

5. **Stress Reduction:** Incorporate stress-reduction techniques such as meditation, deep breathing, or progressive muscle relaxation into your daily routine.

2. Emotional Awareness:

1. **Regular Self-Reflection:** Set aside time for self-reflection to check in with your emotional state.

Journaling is a helpful tool for this purpose.

2. **Emotional Intelligence:** Develop emotional intelligence by working on self-awareness, empathy, and effective communication skills.

3. **Seek Support:** Don't hesitate to seek support from a therapist or counsellor when needed. Professional help can provide valuable insights and tools for managing emotions.

3. Healthy Relationships:

1. **Communication:** Maintain open and honest communication in your relationships. Express your needs and feelings while also actively listening to others.

2. **Boundaries:** Set and enforce healthy boundaries to protect your emotional well-being. Learn to say no when necessary.

3. **Quality Time:** Spend quality time with loved ones, nurturing your relationships and creating positive memories.

4. Stress Management:

1. **Stress Reduction Techniques:** Continuously practice stress reduction techniques to keep stress levels in check. Experiment with various methods to find what works best for you.

2. **Time Management:** Organize your tasks and

responsibilities to reduce unnecessary stress. Prioritize self-care and relaxation.

5. Self-Compassion:

1. **Cultivate Self-Compassion:** Treat yourself with the same kindness and understanding that you offer to others. Embrace self-compassion as a core value.

2. **Positive Self-Talk:** Challenge and replace negative self-talk with positive affirmations and constructive thoughts.

6. Regular Check-Ins:

1. **Self-Assessment:** Periodically assess your emotional health. Are you experiencing any persistent negative emotions or changes in your mood?

2. **Seek Feedback:** Ask for feedback from trusted friends or family members about how they perceive your emotional state and well-being.

3. **Adjust as Needed:** If you identify areas of concern, be proactive in addressing them. Adjust your self-care routine or seek professional support if necessary.

7. Holistic Approaches:

1. **Bach Flower Remedies:** Incorporate Bach Flower Remedies into your long-term emotional health maintenance plan. These remedies can be used preventively to address emerging emotional imbalances.

2. **Mind-Body Practices:** Engage in mind-body practices

like meditation, yoga, or tai chi regularly to promote emotional balance and self-awareness.

8. Community and Support:

1. **Social Connection:** Cultivate a supportive social network. Engage in activities or groups that align with your interests and values.

2. **Therapeutic Groups:** Consider joining therapeutic or support groups that focus on specific emotional challenges or life transitions.

9. Life Purpose and Meaning:

1. **Define Your Values:** Clarify your core values and life purpose. Align your actions with your values to find meaning and fulfilment.

2. **Set Goals:** Set achievable goals that resonate with your values and contribute to your sense of purpose.

10. Celebrate Progress:

1. **Acknowledge Achievements:** Celebrate your successes, no matter how small they may seem. Acknowledging progress reinforces positive emotions.

2. **Practice Gratitude:** Cultivate gratitude by regularly reflecting on the things you're thankful for in your life.

Challenges and Barriers to Long-Term Emotional Health

While the strategies mentioned above can be highly effective, it's important to acknowledge the challenges and potential barriers to maintaining long-term emotional health:

1. **Life Transitions:** Major life changes, such as career shifts, relationship changes, or the loss of a loved one, can significantly impact emotional well-being.

2. **Mental Health Conditions:** Certain mental health conditions may require ongoing management, including medication and therapy.

3. **External Stressors:** External stressors like financial difficulties or environmental factors can challenge emotional stability.

4. **Self-Criticism:** The habit of self-criticism can undermine emotional health. It's important to practice self-compassion and seek support when needed.

Conclusion: A Lifelong Journey of Well-Being

Long-term emotional health is a lifelong journey, and it requires ongoing attention and care. By integrating self-care routines, emotional awareness, healthy relationships, and stress management techniques into your daily life, you can sustain and nurture your emotional well-being. Remember that it's normal to face challenges along the way, and seeking support when needed is a sign of strength and wisdom.

As you embark on this journey, embrace the understanding that emotional well-being is a continuous process of growth and self-discovery. Celebrate your progress, cherish your emotional health, and remember that it is an invaluable asset that empowers you to lead a fulfilling and meaningful life.

Frequently Asked Questions

- Common Queries and Concerns about Bach Flower Remedies

  > **Are Bach Flower Remedies safe to use with other medications or supplements?**

    * Answer: Bach Flower Remedies are generally safe and have no known interactions with medications or supplements. They are considered complementary and can be used alongside other treatments. However, it's a good practice to consult with a healthcare professional, especially if you have concerns.

  > **Can I use Bach Flower Remedies for physical ailments, or are they only for emotional issues?**

    * Answer: Bach Flower Remedies primarily address emotional and mental states. While they may indirectly impact physical well-being by addressing emotional imbalances, they are not a substitute for medical treatment for physical conditions.

  > **How do I know which Bach Flower Remedy is right for me if I have multiple emotional concerns?**

    * Answer: Start with self-awareness. Identify the most dominant or pressing emotional issue you want to address. You can use a single remedy for that issue or consult with a practitioner to create a personalized blend for multiple concerns.

➢ **Are there any side effects or contraindications associated with Bach Flower Remedies?**

* Answer: Bach Flower Remedies are considered safe and have no known side effects or contraindications. They are non-toxic and non-addictive.

➢ **How long does it take to see results when using Bach Flower Remedies?**

* Answer: The time varies from person to person. Some people may experience immediate relief, while for others, it may take several weeks. Consistency in use is key to seeing results.

➢ **Can I give Bach Flower Remedies to my children or pets?**

* Answer: Yes, Bach Flower Remedies are safe for children and pets. You can administer them by adding drops to their drinking water food or applying them to their skin.

➢ **Is it possible to overdose on Bach Flower Remedies?**

* Answer: Bach Flower Remedies are extremely dilute and safe to use. There is no risk of overdose. You can take them as frequently as needed.

➢ **Can I use Bach Flower Remedies during pregnancy or while breastfeeding?**

* Answer: Bach Flower Remedies are generally considered safe during pregnancy and breastfeeding. However, it's advisable to consult with a healthcare provider for personalized guidance.

➤ **Do Bach Flower Remedies have a shelf life or expiration date?**

* Answer: Bach Flower Remedies have a long shelf life and do not typically expire. However, it's best to check the label for any specific instructions.

➤ **Can Bach Flower Remedies be used preventatively, or are they only for acute issues?**

* Answer: Bach Flower Remedies can be used both preventatively and for acute issues. They are versatile and can support emotional balance in various situations.

➤ **What is the role of a Bach Flower practitioner, and how can I find one?**

* Answer: A Bach Flower practitioner is trained to assess your emotional state and recommend specific remedies. You can find a practitioner through Bach Flower organizations or directories.

➤ **How do I store Bach Flower Remedies to ensure their effectiveness?**

* Answer: Store Bach Flower Remedies in a cool, dark place away from direct sunlight and strong odours. Avoid touching the dropper to your mouth to prevent contamination.

➤ **What is the difference between Rescue Remedy and other Bach Flower Remedies?**

* Answer: Rescue Remedy is a combination of five Bach Flower Remedies designed for immediate relief in times of stress or crisis. Other Bach Remedies target specific emotions or personality traits.

➤ **Are there any scientific studies that support the effectiveness of Bach Flower Remedies?**

* Answer: While scientific research on Bach Flower Remedies is limited, some studies and anecdotal evidence suggest their potential benefits for emotional well-being.

➤ **Can Bach Flower Remedies be used in combination with other holistic therapies like acupuncture or aromatherapy?**

* Answer: Yes, Bach Flower Remedies can complement other holistic therapies. They are non-invasive and can be integrated into a holistic wellness plan.

➤ **What do I do if I'm not sure which emotion I'm experiencing or how to describe it accurately?**

* Answer: Bach Flower practitioners are skilled at helping individuals identify their emotions. You can also explore remedies for common emotional states and see which resonates with you.

➢ **Are Bach Flower Remedies suitable for long-term use, or should they be used only temporarily?**

* Answer: Bach Flower Remedies can be used for both short-term and long-term emotional support. They are non-habit-forming and gentle.

➢ **How can I incorporate Bach Flower Remedies into my daily routine for ongoing emotional support?**

* Answer: You can add Bach Flower Remedies to your daily routine by taking them in water, applying them topically, or using a combination bottle. Consistency is key.

➢ **What should I do if I experience a strong emotional reaction or intensification of emotions when using a Bach Flower Remedy?**

* Answer: This can be a sign that the remedy is working. Allow yourself to process the emotions, and consult with a practitioner if needed for guidance.

> ➤ **Are there any dietary or lifestyle recommendations to complement the use of Bach Flower Remedies for emotional balance?**
>
>> * Answer: Maintaining a healthy lifestyle with balanced nutrition, regular exercise, relaxation techniques, and mindfulness can complement the effects of Bach Flower Remedies on emotional well-being.

Please note that while Bach Flower Remedies are generally considered safe, it's essential to consult with a healthcare professional or Bach Flower practitioner for personalized guidance, especially if you have specific health concerns or are using them in conjunction with other treatments.

- **Addressing Safety, Efficacy, and Interactions**

Bach Flower Remedies, a system of natural flower essences developed by Dr. Edward Bach in the early 20th century, have gained popularity for their holistic approach to emotional well-being. These remedies are often used to address a wide range of emotional and psychological concerns, but questions about their safety, efficacy, and potential interactions with other treatments commonly arise. In this article, we will explore these key aspects of Bach Flower Remedies to provide a comprehensive understanding of their use.

Safety of Bach Flower Remedies

One of the primary reasons for the widespread use of Bach Flower Remedies is their excellent safety profile. They are considered safe for almost everyone, including infants, children, adults, and even pets. Here are some key points regarding the safety of Bach Flower Remedies:

1. **Non-Toxic:** Bach Flower Remedies are extremely diluted preparations, containing only trace amounts of the original flower material. They are non-toxic and do not pose a risk of overdose.

2. **No Known Side Effects:** Bach Flower Remedies do not have known side effects when used as directed.

3. **Compatibility:** Bach Flower Remedies are compatible with other forms of treatment, including conventional medicine, homoeopathy, and other holistic therapies. They do not interfere with the action of medications or other supplements.

4. **No Dependency:** These remedies are non-addictive. Using them over time does not lead to dependency or reduced effectiveness.

5. **Safe During Pregnancy and Breastfeeding:** Bach Flower Remedies are generally considered safe for pregnant and breastfeeding individuals. However, it's advisable to consult with a healthcare provider before use.

6. **Minimal Contraindications:** There are very few contraindications for Bach Flower Remedies. However, individuals with severe alcohol sensitivities may need to be cautious since the remedies are preserved in brandy.

Efficacy of Bach Flower Remedies

While the safety of Bach Flower Remedies is well-established, questions about their effectiveness often arise. It's important to understand that Bach Flower Remedies work on the principle of addressing emotional and mental imbalances, and their efficacy can be subjective. Here are key points regarding their effectiveness:

1. **Individual Variability:** The response to Bach Flower Remedies varies from person to person. What works effectively for one individual may not produce the same results for another. This is because the remedies are selected based on an individual's unique emotional state.

2. **Self-awareness:** Self-awareness is crucial when using Bach Flower Remedies. It's essential to accurately identify and describe your emotional state or concerns to select the most appropriate remedies.

3. **Consistency and Patience:** The effects of Bach Flower Remedies may not be immediate. It often takes time and consistent use to see noticeable changes in emotional well-being.

4. **Holistic Approach:** Bach Flower Remedies are best suited for those who embrace a holistic approach to well-being. They are not a quick fix but rather a tool for promoting emotional balance within the context of a balanced lifestyle.

5. **Scientific Research:** While there is limited scientific

research on Bach Flower Remedies, some studies and anecdotal evidence suggest their potential benefits for emotional well-being. However, more research is needed to establish their efficacy conclusively.

Interactions with Other Treatments

A common concern when using holistic remedies like Bach Flower Essences is their potential interactions with other treatments. Here's what you need to know:

1. **Complementary Use:** Bach Flower Remedies are often used alongside conventional medicine, homoeopathy, and other holistic therapies. They are considered complementary and do not typically interfere with the action of medications or other treatments.

2. **Consultation with Healthcare Providers:** It's advisable to inform your healthcare provider about your use of Bach Flower Remedies, especially if you are undergoing medical treatment. While interactions are rare, healthcare professionals should be aware of all therapies you are using.

3. **Compatibility with Holistic Therapies:** Bach Flower Remedies can complement other holistic treatments like acupuncture, aromatherapy, and energy healing. They are seen as part of a holistic approach to well-being.

4. **Personalized Approach:** The selection of Bach Flower Remedies is highly personalized and based on an

individual's emotional state. Practitioners consider the whole person and their unique needs when recommending remedies.

5. **No Known Negative Interactions:** There are no known negative interactions between Bach Flower Remedies and medications or other holistic therapies. However, it's essential to maintain open communication with your healthcare providers.

Bach Flower Remedies offers a safe and holistic approach to addressing emotional imbalances. Their safety profile, minimal contraindications, and compatibility with other treatments make them accessible to a wide range of individuals seeking emotional support. While their effectiveness may vary from person to person, many individuals have reported positive outcomes in their emotional well-being. As with any form of holistic therapy, consistency, self-awareness, and open communication with healthcare providers are key to a successful Bach Flower Remedies experience.

Chapter : 10

Resources and References

- Recommended Books, Websites, and Other Resources

As you explore the world of Bach Flower Remedies and seek to deepen your understanding and knowledge, it's important to have access to reputable and informative resources. In this section, we provide a curated list of recommended books, websites, and other valuable resources to help you on your journey with Bach Flower Remedies.

Books on Bach Flower Remedies

"The Bach Flower Remedies" by Dr. Edward Bach - Start with the source! Dr. Edward Bach's book provides insight into his philosophy and individual remedies. It's a foundational text for understanding the remedies.

1. **"The Bach Remedies Workbook" by Stefan Ball and Judy Howard** - A practical guide that delves into the remedies, their applications, and case studies. It's an excellent resource for both beginners and experienced users.

2. **"Bach Flower Therapy: Theory and Practice" by Mechthild Scheffer** - A comprehensive guide that covers the remedies' history, preparation, and applications. It includes case studies and practical advice.

3. **"Bach Flower Essences and Chinese Medicine" by Pablo Noriega and Mechthild Scheffer** - This book explores the connection between Bach Flower Remedies and traditional Chinese medicine, offering a

unique perspective on emotional healing.

4.   **"The Bach Flower Remedies Step by Step" by Judy Howard** - A user-friendly guide that breaks down the selection process and usage of Bach Flower Remedies in various situations.

Websites and Online Resources

The Bach Centre (www.bachcentre.com): The official website of the Bach Centre provides extensive information about Dr. Edward Bach, the history of Bach Flower Remedies, and a database of the remedies and their indications.

1.   **Bach Flower Essence Society (www.bachflowersociety. org):** This organization offers resources, publications, and educational materials related to Bach Flower Remedies. They also host events and workshops.

2.   **Flower Essence Society (www.flowersociety.org):** While not exclusive to Bach Flower Remedies, this site provides valuable information about flower essences in general, including research and educational resources.

3.   **Bach Flower Reference Guide (www.bachflower. com):** An online resource that provides detailed information about each Bach Flower Remedy, including indications, emotional states, and usage guidelines.

4.   **Bach Flower Quiz (www.bachflowerquiz.com):** A fun and interactive online quiz that can help you identify which Bach Flower Remedies may be most relevant to your current emotional state.

Online Forums and Communities

1. **Bach Flower Remedies Facebook Group:** Joining a Facebook group dedicated to Bach Flower Remedies can be a great way to connect with others, share experiences, and seek advice.

2. **Bach Flower Essence Forum (www.bachflowerforum.com):** An online forum where users of Bach Flower Remedies discuss their experiences and offer support and guidance to one another.

Bach Flower Practitioners and Courses

1. **Find a Practitioner:** Consider working with a Bach Flower practitioner for personalized guidance. The Bach Centre and other organizations often have directories of certified practitioners.

2. **Bach Flower Courses:** If you're interested in deepening your knowledge and becoming a certified practitioner yourself, many organizations offer online and in-person courses and training programs.

Research Articles and Journals

While there may not be a wealth of scientific research on Bach Flower Remedies, some journals and articles explore their effects and potential benefits. You can find relevant studies in psychology, complementary and alternative medicine, and holistic health journals.

Local Health Food Stores and Practitioners

Many local health food stores and holistic health practitioners may carry Bach Flower Remedies and offer guidance on their use. These individuals can be valuable resources for personalized advice.

Online Retailers

You can purchase Bach Flower Remedies from reputable online retailers. Be sure to choose reliable sources that provide clear product information and have positive customer reviews.

In summary, Bach Flower Remedies offer a holistic and natural approach to emotional well-being, and there are numerous resources available to support your journey with these remedies. Whether you're a beginner looking for introductory materials or an experienced practitioner seeking to deepen your knowledge, the recommended books, websites, and other resources listed here can be valuable assets. Remember that learning and working with Bach Flower Remedies is a personal and evolving process, so don't hesitate to explore, ask questions, and seek guidance as needed.

- Glossary of Terms and Definitions

    1. **Bach Flower Remedies**: A system of natural flower essences developed by Dr. Edward Bach to address emotional imbalances and promote emotional well-being.

    2. **Remedy:** A specific Bach Flower Essence used to

address particular emotional states or personality traits.

3. **Bach Centre:** The organization founded by Dr. Edward Bach to promote and preserve his work and teachings on Bach Flower Remedies.

4. **Essence:** The energetic and vibrational imprint of a flower or plant, which is transferred to water to create a Bach Flower Remedy.

5. **Dilution:** The process of mixing a few drops of a Bach Flower Essence with spring water, which serves as the method of administration.

6. **Materia Medica:** A comprehensive reference guide or database that provides detailed information about each Bach Flower Remedy, including its indications, characteristics, and uses.

7. **Indications:** The specific emotional states, behaviours, or personality traits that a Bach Flower Remedy is designed to address.

8. **Selection:** The process of choosing the appropriate Bach Flower Remedy based on an individual's emotional state or symptoms.

9. **Personal Blend:** A customized combination of Bach Flower Remedies created to address multiple emotional issues simultaneously.

10. **Rescue Remedy:** A combination of five Bach Flower

Remedies (Cherry Plum, Clematis, Impatiens, Rock Rose, and Star of Bethlehem) used for immediate relief in times of acute stress, anxiety, or crisis.

11. **Bottle Method:** A method of administering Bach Flower Remedies by adding a few drops of the selected remedy to a glass bottle of spring water for regular sipping throughout the day.

12. **Direct Application:** The practice of applying Bach Flower Remedies directly to the skin or pulse points, often in the form of a mist or lotion.

13. **Combination Bottle:** A bottle containing a combination of Bach Flower Remedies, usually created by adding a few drops of each selected remedy to a glass bottle of water.

14. **Dose:** The quantity of Bach Flower Remedy taken at one time, typically consisting of a few drops in the chosen method of administration.

- Bibliography of Research Papers and Scientific Articles

<u>**Chapter : 11**</u>

Conclusion

- Recap of Key Points and Takeaways

Conclusion: Recap and Final Thoughts on Bach Flower Remedies

In this comprehensive guide, we've explored the world of Bach Flower Remedies, a natural and gentle approach to emotional and mental well-being. From understanding the philosophy behind these remedies to selecting the right one for specific emotional states, and from methods of administration to dosage guidelines, we've covered all the essential aspects of using Bach Flower Remedies effectively. As we conclude, let's recap the key points and takeaways and offer some final thoughts and encouragement for readers interested in incorporating these remedies into their lives.

Recap of Key Points and Takeaways

1. **Bach Flower Remedies Philosophy:** Bach Flower Remedies, developed by Dr. Edward Bach, are based on the belief that emotional imbalances can contribute to physical illnesses. These remedies aim to address specific emotional states and promote overall well-being.

2. **Understanding the Remedies:** There are 38 different Bach Flower Remedies, each targeting specific emotions or personality traits. Understanding the indications and characteristics of each remedy is essential for selecting the right one.

3. **Choosing the Right Remedy:** To choose the right Bach

Flower Remedy, begin with self-awareness. Identify the emotions or behaviours you want to address, and then select the remedy that resonates with your current situation.

4. **Methods of Administration:** Bach Flower Remedies can be administered orally by adding drops to water, through direct application to the skin, as combination bottles, in topical creams or lotions, and even via inhalation.

5. **Dosage Guidelines:** The frequency and duration of Bach Flower Remedies can vary depending on the individual and the specific emotional issue. The recommended dosage typically involves taking the remedy at least four times a day until a positive change is observed.

6. **Combining Remedies:** You can create personalized blends of Bach Flower Remedies by combining up to seven remedies to address multiple emotional issues simultaneously.

7. **Rescue Remedy:** In times of acute stress or crisis, Rescue Remedy, a combination of five remedies, can provide immediate relief when taken directly under the tongue or added to water.

8. **Children and Pets:** Bach Flower Remedies are safe for children and pets. You can administer them by adding drops to their drinking water food or applying them to their skin.

Final Thoughts and Encouragement for Readers

Using Bach Flower Remedies can be a transformative and empowering experience on your journey to emotional and mental well-being. As we wrap up, here are some final thoughts and encouragement for those interested in incorporating these remedies into their lives:

Trust the Process: Bach Flower Remedies work gently and gradually. It may take some time before you notice significant changes in your emotional state. Trust the process, and be patient with yourself.

Self-Awareness: Bach Flower Remedies provide a unique opportunity for self-reflection and self-awareness. By identifying your emotions and addressing them with the appropriate remedy, you can gain deeper insight into your inner world.

Holistic Approach: Consider adopting a holistic approach to emotional well-being. Bach Flower Remedies can complement other wellness practices such as meditation, mindfulness, yoga, and therapy. These approaches can work synergistically to support your overall health.

Consult a Practitioner: While Bach Flower Remedies are user-friendly and safe, consulting with a Bach Flower practitioner can provide valuable insights and personalized guidance. Practitioners can help you create custom blends tailored to your specific needs.

Embrace Self-Care: Incorporate self-care practices into your daily routine. Taking time for self-care activities like relaxation, exercise, and spending time in nature can enhance the effectiveness of Bach Flower Remedies.

Maintain an Open Mind: Keep an open mind and allow yourself to explore the subtle yet powerful effects of Bach Flower Remedies. Their gentle nature means they can be used alongside other healing modalities without interference.

Journal Your Journey: Keeping a journal can be a powerful tool for tracking your emotional progress while using Bach Flower Remedies. Document your thoughts, feelings, and observations as you take the remedies. This can help you gain clarity and perspective on your emotional growth.

Seek Professional Help When Needed: While Bach Flower Remedies can be beneficial for managing everyday emotional concerns, they are not a substitute for professional medical or psychological treatment. If you are dealing with severe or persistent emotional issues, consider seeking guidance from a qualified healthcare provider or therapist.

Share Your Experiences: As you experience the benefits of Bach Flower Remedies, consider sharing your knowledge and experiences with friends and family who may also benefit from these remedies. Spreading awareness can positively impact the emotional well-being of your loved ones.

Continual Learning: Bach Flower Remedies offer a rich field of study and exploration. Continue learning about these remedies and their applications. There is always more to discover and understand about their potential to support emotional healing.

Bach Flower Remedies are a valuable and accessible resource for those seeking emotional balance and well-being. By embracing these gentle remedies and integrating them into your life with mindfulness and self-compassion, you can embark on a transformative journey towards greater emotional harmony and personal growth. Remember that your emotional well-being is a lifelong journey, and Bach Flower Remedies can be a supportive companion along the way.

Bach Flower Remedies: The Healing Power of Nature for Emotional Balance

In today's fast-paced and often stressful world, many people seek natural and holistic approaches to achieve emotional balance and well-being. Bach Flower Remedies, a system of natural healing developed by Dr. Edward Bach in the early 20th century, offer a unique and gentle way to address emotional and mental health concerns. With their roots deeply embedded in the healing power of flowers and plants, Bach Flower Remedies provide individuals with an alternative path to emotional healing and personal growth.

The Origins of Bach Flower Remedies

Dr. Edward Bach, a British physician and homoeopath, is the visionary behind Bach Flower Remedies. Born in 1886, Bach was a physician with a keen interest in nature and holistic medicine. His journey to developing the Bach Flower Remedies began with a desire to find a natural and gentle way to address emotional and psychological imbalances, believing that emotional disharmony was at the root of many physical illnesses.

Over several years of research and exploration, Dr. Bach discovered 38 different flower essences, each of which resonated with specific emotional states. He believed that these essences, when prepared and administered correctly, could help restore emotional equilibrium, thus promoting overall health. These remedies are often referred to as "vibrational" or "energy" medicines because they work on an energetic level to address imbalances in emotions.

Understanding the Philosophy of Bach Flower Remedies

The core philosophy of Bach Flower Remedies is based on the belief that emotional and mental states have a profound impact on physical health. Dr. Bach saw our emotional well-being as interconnected with our physical health and believed that by addressing emotional imbalances, the body's natural healing abilities could be stimulated.

Each of the 38 Bach Flower Remedies is associated with a specific emotional state or personality trait. For example, the remedy "Mimulus" is used for those experiencing fear of known things, while "Agrimony" is recommended for individuals who hide their inner turmoil behind a cheerful facade. The idea is to select remedies that align with the emotional issues a person is facing.

The Process of Preparing Bach Flower Remedies

The preparation of Bach Flower Remedies is a meticulous and labour-intensive process that Dr. Bach himself developed. It involves collecting dewdrops from the flowers early in the morning when they are at their most potent. These dewdrops are then preserved in a solution of water and alcohol to create the flower essences.

The flower essences are further diluted to create the final remedies that are readily available to the public. The dilution process ensures that the remedies are safe and suitable for use by individuals of all ages, including children and pets.

How Bach Flower Remedies are Administered

One of the great advantages of Bach Flower Remedies is their ease of use. They can be administered in several ways, making them accessible to a wide range of individuals. The most common methods of administration include:

1. **Direct Oral Ingestion:** This is the simplest method, where a few drops of the selected Bach Flower Remedy are placed under the tongue or diluted in water and sipped throughout the day. The remedies are typically taken two to four times a day.

2. **Topical Application:** In some cases, the remedies can be applied topically by diluting them in a carrier oil and massaging them onto the skin. This method is often used for emotional issues related to skin conditions or localized discomfort.

3. **Incorporation in Daily Routine:** Some individuals choose to add a few drops of Bach Flower Remedies to their bathwater, moisturizers, or room sprays to infuse their daily environment with the vibrational energy of the remedies.

4.   **Combination Remedies:** In addition to individual remedies, Bach Flower Remedies can also be found in pre-made combinations designed to address specific emotional themes, such as stress relief or confidence-building.

The Gentle Nature of Bach Flower Remedies

One of the most appealing aspects of Bach Flower Remedies is their gentle and non-invasive nature. They do not interfere with other forms of medication or treatment and are considered safe for most people, including pregnant women, children, and the elderly.

Unlike some conventional medications that may suppress or mask symptoms, Bach Flower Remedies work by helping individuals confront and transform their emotional issues at their roots. The goal is to promote self-awareness and emotional growth rather than simply alleviating symptoms.

Conditions Addressed by Bach Flower Remedies

Bach Flower Remedies can be used to address a wide range of emotional and psychological concerns. Some common areas where they can be beneficial include:

1.   **Anxiety and Stress:** Remedies like "Rescue Remedy" are often used for immediate relief from stress and anxiety. Others like "Rock Rose" and "Agrimony" target specific aspects of these emotions.

2.   **Fear and Phobias:** Whether it's fear of heights, fear of public speaking, or any other type of phobia, there are

Bach Flower Remedies tailored to address these specific fears.

3. **Grief and Loss:** Emotional pain associated with the loss of a loved one or a significant life change can be eased with remedies like "Star of Bethlehem" and "Honeysuckle."

4. **Low Self-Esteem and Confidence:** Remedies like "Larch" and "Crab Apple" can help boost self-esteem and self-worth.

5. **Relationship Issues:** Bach Flower Remedies can also be used to address conflicts and emotional challenges in relationships, promoting better communication and understanding.

6. **Negative Thoughts and Obsessions:** Individuals struggling with persistent negative thoughts or obsessions can benefit from remedies like "White Chestnut" and "Cherry Plum."

It's important to note that while Bach Flower Remedies can be a valuable complement to emotional healing, they are not a substitute for medical or psychological treatment in cases of severe mental illness or trauma. They are best used as part of a holistic approach to wellness.

Personalized Treatment with Bach Flower Remedies

One of the unique features of Bach Flower Remedies is their individualized approach. Rather than a one-size-fits-all solution, the remedies are tailored to the specific emotional and mental state of each person. This makes them a highly customizable and personalized form of treatment.

To determine which Bach Flower Remedies are most suitable for an individual, practitioners often conduct an in-depth consultation. During this consultation, individuals are encouraged to express their emotions, fears, and concerns. The practitioner then selects the remedies that best match the person's emotional profile.

The Role of Practitioners in Bach Flower Therapy

While some individuals choose to self-prescribe Bach Flower Remedies based on their own research and understanding of their emotional state, it is often advisable to seek the guidance of a trained Bach Flower practitioner. These practitioners have a deep understanding of the remedies and can provide personalized recommendations based on their expertise.

A Bach Flower practitioner can help individuals explore their emotions, identify underlying issues, and select the appropriate remedies for their unique needs. This guidance can enhance the effectiveness of the remedies and promote a deeper level of healing.

Scientific Research and Efficacy of Bach Flower Remedies

Bach Flower Remedies have been the subject of various studies and research initiatives to assess their efficacy. While the scientific evidence is still evolving and more research is needed, some studies have shown promising results in support of Bach Flower Remedies' ability to improve emotional well-being.

For example, a study published in the journal "Complementary

Therapies in Medicine" in 2019 explored the effects of Bach Flower Remedies on psychological well-being. The researchers found that participants who received Bach Flower Remedies reported improvements in emotional balance and quality of life.

Another study, published in the "Journal of Alternative and Complementary Medicine" in 2013, investigated the effects of Bach Flower Remedies on stress and anxiety. The results suggested that Bach Flower Remedies, when used as part of a holistic approach, can help reduce stress and anxiety levels in individuals.

It's important to note that more rigorous scientific research is needed to establish the full scope of Bach Flower Remedies' effectiveness and mechanisms of action. However, the anecdotal evidence and positive experiences of many individuals who have used these remedies highlight their potential as a complementary approach to emotional healing.

Conclusion: Embracing the Healing Power of Flowers

Bach Flower Remedies offers a gentle and holistic approach to emotional healing and personal growth. Rooted in the belief that emotional well-being is integral to overall health, these remedies harness the vibrational energy of flowers to address a wide range of emotional concerns.

While Bach Flower Remedies are not a replacement for medical or psychological treatment in serious cases, they can play a valuable role in promoting emotional balance and self-awareness. Their individualized nature, ease of use, and gentle approach make them accessible to people of all ages and backgrounds.

As you embark on your journey of emotional healing and self-discovery, consider exploring the healing power of flowers through Bach Flower Remedies. Whether you seek relief from stress anxiety, or a deeper understanding of your emotions, these remedies may offer a path to greater emotional well-being and a more harmonious life.

Remember that your emotional well-being is a journey, and Bach Flower Remedies can be a supportive companion on that path. Embrace the wisdom of nature and the potential for growth and transformation that these remedies offer. Just as flowers bloom and evolve, so too can you flourish in emotional balance and well-being with the gentle guidance of Bach Flower Remedies.

.This extended article provides a comprehensive overview of Bach Flower Remedies, their origins, philosophy, administration, conditions they can address, personalized treatment, the role of practitioners, scientific research, and their potential for emotional healing and personal growth.

About Author

Supriya Salve, an emotional mastery coach, embarked on the journey of writing her book, **"The Healing Power of Flowers: Exploring Bach Flower Remedies,"** with a heartfelt intention to make a positive impact on the lives of many individuals. Her motivation stems from the belief in the profound ability of Bach Flower Remedies to heal emotional and psychological imbalances.

Through her extensive knowledge and expertise, Supriya aims to empower and educate her readers on the transformative potential of these remedies. She envisions helping people discover the healing properties of various flowers and their application in promoting emotional well-being.

In today's fast-paced and often stressful world, many individuals grapple with emotional challenges. Supriya's book serves as a beacon of hope, offering natural and holistic solutions to navigate these emotional complexities. By sharing insights and practical guidance, she aspires to enable her readers to embark on a journey of self-discovery and emotional healing.

Supriya Salve's book is a testament to her commitment to making a difference in the lives of those seeking emotional balance and personal transformation. Her work provides a valuable resource that not only educates but also inspires individuals to harness the healing power of flowers to lead more fulfilling and harmonious lives.

9 789360 062811